CW00460470

Come Hill and High Water

A lifetime of adventure, climbing and sailing

Tom Dutton

APRIL SNOW IN CWM IDWAL, A PAINTING BY DAVID WOODFORD

The painting captures, in an almost magical way, the play of light on mountains lightly dressed with snow.

First published in July 2010; this revised edition published in November 2012 by B. Dutton Publishing Limited, The Grange, Hones Yard, Farnham, Surrey, GU9 8BB.

Copyright: Thomas E Dutton 2010–2012

ISBN-13: 978-1-905113-44-6

Publisher: Beverley Dutton

Group Editor: Jenny Stewart

Editors: Becky Breuer and Jenny Royle

Copy Editor: Amy Norman

Editorial Assistants: Adele Duthie and Frankie New

Art Director/Designer: Sarah Ryan

Graphic Designer: Louise Pepé

Designer: Zena Deakin

PR and Advertising Manager: Natalie Bull

Printed in Slovenia

Cover image: A party on the summit of the Matterhorn about to begin the descent to Zermatt

Foreword

There are no two ways about it: Tom Dutton is a phenomenon. While most folk of his age would have long since led a sedentary life, Tom has taken his by the scruff of its neck and continued to relish it. His experiences are legion and his way of describing them enriching.

Come Hill and High Water is an engaging account of climbing experiences and encounters – with both mountains and the people who attempt to scale them. Why climb a mountain? If your only answer is the oft-quoted 'because it's there' then Tom's book will give you other reasons. He has an eye for beauty and a dry sense of humour, and I only wish I could have shared in some of his experiences. Imagine his face, halfway up a mountain, when, 'I was overtaken by a girl also with a rope slung round her shoulders but somewhat oddly dressed, I thought, for she was wearing a rather stylish summer frock.'

Not just 'a summer frock', you notice, but 'a rather stylish summer frock'. Tom notices things – whether it is stylish frocks or mountains enveloped in a skein of mist. His book will entertain and inspire you in equal measure. The only trouble is, it might also make your own adventures seem a little bit tame.

Alan Titchmarsh MBE

Dedication and Acknowledgements

To the memory of Phyl, who kept the home fires burning, and to all the staunch friends with whom I had the pleasure of sharing rope and tiller.

I must also thank, most warmly, my shipmates Ivan Barnett, Richard Barrett, Ron McGregor and Ray O'Neill, who went painstakingly through my draft and made a number of very helpful suggestions.

Then I must record how very grateful I am to Becky Breuer for the meticulous way in which she edited the book and generally tidied up the text, including 'pepping up' some of my more old-fashioned phraseology where required.

The splendid photograph of Richard Barrett on Helvellyn, page 108, was taken by Ivan Barnett and the fine picture of the Cioch on page 111 was taken by Ron McGregor. The remaining photographs are from the author's own collection.

I should, perhaps, point out that, although this book is intended to encourage people to venture into high places and deep waters, it is a book of reminiscences and not a climber's or walker's guide or a yachtsman's pilot. Neither the author nor the publisher can, therefore, accept responsibility for any errors or omissions which may have crept in and remained undetected.

Introduction

Since it is customary to say something about how a book came to be written, I must mention that this one was the result of a chance remark made by an old climbing friend when my wife, Phyl, and I were celebrating our sixtieth wedding anniversary. We had been talking about the part luck plays in life, when suddenly he said, 'Tom, you really have had the devil's own luck. How many people can say that they have survived one World War, 70 years of mountaineering and 60 years of matrimony, and still be climbing? You really must write a book about it.'

So, more than 70 years since I first climbed Snowdon, I find myself reliving all the exciting things that happened during those years and, I must confess, rather enjoying it. While some of my mountaineering may have been fairly standard when judged against the achievements of the hard men of the day, my companions and I certainly had our moments. The weather, for example, can turn the easiest day into an epic, something we soon discovered when we got caught in a storm on the Eiger.

We had climbed the mountain by the West Flank route and during the ascent the conditions were perfect, but shortly after leaving the summit the weather changed with a violence that would soon have become overwhelming. We realised that we would have to move quickly if we were to get off the mountain alive. The ascent and the descent of the Eiger by the West Flank route, though technically easy, has claimed the lives of many climbers over the years, including a number of very experienced mountaineers who, having climbed the notorious North Wall, were using the West Flank as a quick means of descent. The climbers are tired, everything slopes the wrong way, and a slip is difficult to check.

Another excursion which didn't turn out quite as we had anticipated took place at the other end of the Alps, on a long, classic rock climb in the Dolomites, just above the fashionable ski resort of Cortina. All went well for the first few hundred feet, but as we climbed higher the extreme exposure – the climb is nearly 1,000 feet long, very steep and correspondingly airy – became too much for the leader of our second party, who finally lost his nerve and swore that he couldn't carry on. We thought about abseiling off, but eventually decided to carry on climbing, finishing up with a rope of four, 600 feet of difficult rock still to do, and nightfall fast approaching. We succeeded in completing the climb but were then faced with the problem of getting off the mountain in the dark, which presented some unexpected problems of its own.

Throughout my climbing years, I have always aimed to see as much of the Alps as possible, visiting most of the principal mountain groups, from the Vercors – which is not far from Grenoble – to the Dolomites in northern Italy, and it has been my good fortune to climb many of the major peaks in these regions. Gradually, however, as I reached my mid sixties, I began to concentrate on the lower peaks, especially those in the Italian Alps where the weather is rather better and an early start less crucial.

Back home in the UK, on the other hand, I was packing in more than ever, especially in the first few years after retirement, and a combination of hillwalking and rock climbing took me from the Gower Peninsula in South Wales to the hills of Wester Ross in Scotland, and from the granite sea cliffs of Land's End to the rough gabbro routes on the Isle of Skye. The number of rock climbs my friends and I have enjoyed over the years must run into thousands – including some real gems, which I describe in detail in this book – and I must confess that it is these climbs, rather than the Alpine giants, which I recall with the greatest affection.

The fascination that mountains have for some people is difficult to describe and the excessive risks that mountaineers sometimes take in pursuit of their sport can be hard to justify. It is the same for those who turn to the sea for pleasure: the sailor has no inhibitions when he is pressed to justify the dangers he encounters, and his love of the sea is sufficient to satisfy most people. Looking back with the utmost pleasure on a long lifetime of mountaineering, I can only explain the appeal of the hills in similar terms: it is very deep-rooted. Geoffrey Winthrop Young, the great mountaineer poet, touched on the subject when he wrote:

> There is much comfort in high hills,
>
> And a great easing of the heart.
>
> (*On High Hills*; Methuen, 1927)

Wisely, he didn't attempt to elaborate.

As for sailing, in addition to numerous enjoyable cruises down to Brittany and across to Ireland, I have been lucky enough to be able to spend the best part of three summers helping a friend take his boat out to Greece and back home through the rivers and canals of France. More recently – and well into my seventies by this time – I sailed my own boat, *Vixen*, up to Scotland, accompanied by a number of climbing and sailing companions. We took two summers over the trip: the first, sailing around the Isle of Arran and the adjacent lochs; the second, taking *Vixen* up the west coast of Scotland and around Cape Wrath to the Orkney Islands, before returning to Portsmouth by the west coast of Ireland and the Isles of Scilly. It was a journey which, with all the diversions along the way, totalled nearly 4,000 miles.

If this book encourages young adventurers to follow in my footsteps or in my wake, as the case may be, I will feel that it was well worth writing. But I also hope it will encourage older climbers and sailors to keep going, as most of my alpine climbs – and both the Scottish and the Greek sailing trips – were fitted into a very busy retirement between the ages of 60 and 85. I have certainly been lucky, as mountains are dangerous places, and I describe at least one holiday in this book when my guardian angels must have been keeping a particularly watchful eye on me.

So, let us uncoil the rope, tie on, and start the first pitch.

BACK SAFE AND SOUND
Taking it easy in the Italian Alps.

CHAPTER ONE

What a difference a day makes: luck and near misses

It isn't easy to get climbers to come down from high places and consider the hazards of the sport, but in our more reflective moments we will usually admit that you need a lot of luck in a lifetime of mountaineering if you are to get by without a major mishap of one sort or another.

An accident on Mont Blanc in August 2008, described as one of the worst in decades and in which several climbers were killed, threw a spotlight on one of the major hazards of climbing on all snow-covered mountains, be it in the Alps or in Scotland in winter: the avalanche.

Snow and ice avalanches can vary from the relatively minor hazard, where the contents of a small gully come sliding down, to avalanches of utterly terrifying power and devastation, where the snow and ice covering an entire mountainside hurtle down towards the valley and engulf whole villages. They can be caused by a number of factors but the main one, in most cases, is probably the failure of a fresh fall of snow to bind with the underlying layer of snow or ice. The extra stress of the recent snowfall, a rise in temperature perhaps, or simply the movement of climbers or skiers across the slope can cause the new snow to start to slide.

The sheer scale of some alpine avalanches can be quite unnerving as some friends and I were to discover one summer in Switzerland when we were descending the Rimpfischhorn, a mountain not very far from the Matterhorn. Our route – fortunately, as it turned out – led down a long rock ridge. To our left lay an extensive snowfield, which appeared stable given the fairly moderate incline, and, with the difficulties of our route behind us, we were enjoying an easy descent and the magnificent spectacle of the Matterhorn before us, when our reverie was shattered by a deafening bang. An expanse of the snowfield, the size of several football pitches and ten feet deep, possibly more, began to slide downhill. Quite slowly at first, but quickly gathering devastating momentum, it thundered down the mountainside. We could only hope that there was no one in its path.

Unless you have witnessed the damage first-hand, it is almost impossible to imagine the destructive power of a large avalanche: the force of the air they push before them is itself enough to destroy large trees. Avalanches on this scale are common enough in the Alps but not normally on the routes taken by climbers, as these are especially chosen to avoid such hazards. That day on the Rimpfischhorn, we owed our relative safety to our position on the rock ridge; had the avalanche happened higher up the mountain, the risk would have been far greater.

Avalanches are less frequent in Scotland than in the Alps, but they are now recognized as a more serious threat to winter climbing in Scotland than they were once thought to be. A friend of mine, addicted to winter climbing on Ben Nevis, was carried down various gullies no fewer than five times in 14 years, the last time suffering injuries serious enough to put him into hospital.

Another type of avalanche on mountains with permanent snow occurs when masses of ice break away from the main glacier, often from the glacier snout, and come hurtling down, gathering more snow and ice as they go. Glaciers are essentially rivers of ice and they flow. The rate of flow varies from a few centimetres up to about two metres a day, and the flow is faster at the surface than deeper down, and faster in the middle of the moving channel than at the edges. Since glaciers are usually moving across rough, uneven ground, the ice sheet tends to break up. The resultant cracks, or crevasses, as they are known, sometimes extend right down to the bed of the glacier. If the rocky bed over which the glacier is travelling becomes still more uneven, or if the incline becomes steeper, the ice between the crevasses will separate into slabs or towers known as seracs. Add to this the weakening effect of strong sunlight and the pull of gravity as the seracs tilt, and they will eventually crash down the mountain, sometimes for several thousands of feet, usually breaking up and becoming even more destructive as they go.

Ice avalanches of this kind are a major hazard on the steep ice routes so popular with many climbers today. The most disturbing feature of all types of avalanche is that they can happen at any time and, in most cases, it is impossible to say when. All that you can do to reduce the risk, as with so many mountain-related hazards, is to plan your route carefully, keep your fingers crossed, and hope for the best, moving as quickly as conditions allow. There are, of course, some general precautions you can take and which are part of standard mountaineering practice. An early start is perhaps the most important of these: this way, you should be safely back down and in the hut before the sun gets hot enough to melt the snow and ice, loosening rocks frozen into the upper slopes and causing unstable snow to slide. An early start means just that and, on many major routes, it is normal to be up and out shortly after two o'clock in the morning, doing the first few hours of the route by the light of a head torch.

Another largely unpredictable hazard is the rock avalanche or rockfall. Fortunately, I have only once been on a mountain when a major rockfall occurred, and that was on a little peak in the French Alps close to La

Bérarde. I was with a friend, Brian Shaw, and we had just crossed a gully directly below the summit when a huge rock tower on the crest of the ridge toppled over and came crashing down. What I remember most about the incident was the pungent, sulphurous smell caused as the falling rocks hit the gully walls, rebounding from side to side, many of them shattering in the process. There was nothing we could have done, and we simply thanked our lucky stars that we had crossed the gully when we did.

Again, it is easy to imagine that this sort of thing only happens in the Alps, but there used to be a little pillar of rock known – as are many isolated rock pinnacles – as the Gendarme, which barred the way on a very narrow part of the Cuillin Ridge on the Isle of Skye. Tens of thousands of climbers must have hugged this Scottish Gendarme over the years as they edged round it, very much aware of the considerable drop below. It fell down in the 1980s when, as luck would have it, there was no one about. The most obvious way to avoid these hazards is, of course, simply not to be there at all. As one climber so cleverly put it many years ago:

> On steep mountain faces and perilous places,
>
> I am sure we shall all of us find,
>
> Good climbers and shoddy, that absence of body,
>
> Is better than presence of mind.
>
> (*The Badminton Library: Mountaineering*; Longmans, Green & Co, 1892)

I have had my share of near misses over the years, and two particularly close ones during a brief holiday in the Italian Alps. Like most climbers, I was keen to attempt the Matterhorn and did, in fact, climb the Hörnli Ridge from Zermatt on another occasion during one of my first trips to Switzerland (see Chapter Six, page 51). On this particular holiday, however, our sights were set firmly on the Italian Ridge. I'd met two young climbers – Martin Parry and Martin Barry, both from Sidmouth, I seem to recall – earlier in the holiday and we had agreed to meet at Breuil-Cervinia, where the route starts. We checked with the guides' office whether the conditions were right for an ascent and were told that the Matterhorn was in as good a condition as we were ever likely to get it, and that the weather forecast for the next few days was also good. This was the news we had been hoping for and, feeling quite exhilarated, we set off up the track to the Abruzzi Hut – a substantial hostelry, in fact, and not quite as small as the name 'Hut' might suggest – where we were planning to spend the night before moving up to the Carrel Hut the next morning.

The Abruzzi Hut was crowded, mostly with Spanish climbers, and it was clear we were in for an entertaining evening. Someone was already playing a guitar and no sooner had he finished than an elderly climber began to sing, in a magnificent voice, a series of extracts from Bizet's *Carmen*. But, one by one, we made our way to our bunks, knowing that we would have to make an early start for the Carrel Hut next morning. A good night's sleep is a rare thing on these occasions, and this time I was woken shortly after two in the morning by the noise of rattling windows. I took a look outside and was dismayed to see a blizzard raging: climbing the Matterhorn was almost certainly out of the question.

The mood at breakfast was gloomy and, the meal over, we all traipsed back down to Breuil-Cervinia, disappointed that the climb was off. I wasn't too sure, at first, what to do with the rest of my time. After spending the morning with my companions, looking around the town, I decided to make my way to nearby Aosta, find a comfortable hotel for the night and have a bath.

There was no bus down the valley, so it was either hitch-hiking or a very long walk. I was lucky, and was quickly offered a lift by a driver who turned out to be a local guide who regularly took climbers up the Matterhorn. When I told him that we had been poised to move up from the Abruzzi Hut to the Carrel Hut that morning, he looked very serious and remarked how lucky we had been, adding that there would be no climbing on the Matterhorn for at least a fortnight.

Ten days later one of the national newspapers back home in the UK reported that the climbers trapped in the Carrel Hut had been airlifted off the mountain. The hut, at about 12,500 feet, is approximately 2,000 feet below the summit of the Matterhorn (14,692 feet) and I'm told that it is very basic, very cold and that the only food available is what you have with you. No place for a picnic! Whenever I think about the Italian Ridge on the Matterhorn and how we might have been among those airlifted to safety, that catchy little tune 'What a difference a day makes, twenty-four little hours ...' starts playing in my head.

At Aosta, I was out of luck again. For almost two hours, I tried hotel after hotel, but there were no rooms to be had. Aosta, an attractive city with some fine relics of Imperial Rome, was obviously very popular with tourists and it was the height of the holiday season. I wasn't too worried at this point, however. I was confident that, as a last resort, I would be able to get a bus to one of the villages in the hills to the south of the city and find somewhere to sleep there.

I tried one or two more hotels in Aosta, then found the bus station and took the first bus to a village about ten miles south. But here it was the same story. Five hotels in the village and as many pensioni, but nothing doing. Suspecting that they were putting me off in the hope that they might fill any available room with a couple and at a higher rate, I explained that I was quite willing to pay for a double room if that would help. My suspicions seemed justified when one hotelier, obviously very amused with himself, replied, 'Yes, but you won't eat two dinners or drink two bottles of wine.'

So, in spite of my efforts, it looked like yet another night in the tent. This didn't worry me particularly, but I had been looking forward to a hot bath and I wasn't sure where I would be able to camp as there was no official camp-site and the sides of the valley were heavily wooded and very steep. For two hours, I plodded onwards feeling increasingly fed up as the valley closed menacingly in around me. Since leaving the village behind, the only living things I had seen were three cyclists who shot past me singing their heads off.

After a while, the daylight began to fade and it wasn't long before I had to switch on my head torch. I'd had quite enough by this time. But then, at last and to my great relief, I spotted a little track leading off to the left that looked as if it might lead to level ground. It did, but the terrain was very rocky and there was a pungent, slightly sulphurous smell about the place. By now, I was far too tired to worry about what this smell might imply and, after pitching the tent, was soon fast asleep.

I must have slept well in spite of the rocky ground, because it was broad daylight by the time I woke up. In fact, I might have slept even longer had it not been for the noise of heavy machinery working nearby. It was then that I remembered the sulphurous smell and all the rocks lying about the place, and I was up and out of bed in a shot: I had spent the night in the middle of a landslide! The rocks had obviously crashed down from the mountain above and had torn away a short stretch of the road; the sound of heavy machinery turned out to be a digger trying to make some sort of track across the debris. Just below my tent was an ugly jumble of rocks and a few shattered pine trees. When I spoke to the man operating the digger, he told me that the landslide had happened about 24 hours previously, fortunately with no loss of life. 'What a difference a day makes, twenty-four little hours …'!

THE DEVIL'S SLIDE
A classic slab climb on the island of Lundy in the Bristol Channel

A DAY IN CWM GLAS MAWR

We climbed The Parson's Nose and
The Gambit, some 40 years after I first
climbed them. The Parson's Nose is the
steep ridge in the background.

CHAPTER TWO

Early days

My climbing days began at the age of 14 when I persuaded a school friend, Norman Rickard, to cycle with me to North Wales during the Easter holidays with the intention of climbing Snowdon. At the time, I didn't know any climbers, and had got the idea from the local library, where I enjoyed the books of George and Ashley Abraham, photographer brothers who climbed in the Lake District. What may seem a very adventurous expedition for young boys now was probably fairly normal in those days, and we weren't particularly worried about what we were taking on at the time. But the ride from St Helens in South Lancashire, where we lived, to Snowdonia is still a pretty long one, especially at that age, and after Chester we began to find that grinding away, our bikes weighed down with the very heavy camping gear of the time, was more than we had bargained for.

We struggled on a bit further and when we reached Llangollen, and liked the look of the place, we decided we had gone far enough. After looking at one or two camp-sites near the town, we decided that they weren't what we wanted, so we pushed our bikes to the top of Dinas Bran and camped there for the night. Dinas Bran was hardly Snowdon but it is a high enough hill, with more impressive hills all around, so on the whole we felt we hadn't done too badly. We set off on the 50-mile ride home the following day feeling tired but satisfied – for the time being.

By the following summer, we had toughened up a lot, and Norman and I set off once again for North Wales, determined at least to see Snowdon even if we didn't climb it. We must have got much fitter in the few months since Easter, because this time we went via Mold and Denbigh, and the stretch of road from Denbigh across the moors, until you drop down into the Conwy Valley, is particularly hilly. We were slow crossing the moors

– it was hard going – but once across them we had miles of free-wheeling to take our minds off how tired we were. The grind up to Capel Curig and pushing the bikes up the steep road to Pen-y-Pass was exhausting work, but it was two happy teenagers who camped at the foot of Snowdon that night – we had reached real mountains at last!

Early the following morning, we set off up the track from Pen-y-Pass and soon had the summit of Snowdon in view. From there to the summit itself, driven as we were by curiosity and excitement, seemed to take no more than a matter of minutes. I have been on the summit countless times since that first day and remember many of the occasions clearly, but none has left quite as deep an impression as that very first day on Snowdon, looking out across the Glaslyn estuary.

I can remember very little of the rest of this trip, apart from camping in a farmer's field at Aber for which we were charged sixpence for the night – hardly anything these days, but a lot of money to schoolboys in those days, who thought they were lucky if they got any pocket money at all!

The expedition the following summer was my first real climbing trip. My father had given me the train ticket to Betws-y-Coed and, encouraged by what I had read in Carr and Lister's *The Mountains of Snowdonia* (The Bodley Head, 1925) and the various books by the Abraham brothers, I trudged through Betws-y-Coed bound for Pen-y-Pass, with a vague idea that I would be able to find accommodation at one of the cottages near the hotel, which then functioned at the top of the Pass. For a while, the weather just about held its own, but as I left Capel Curig it began to rain, getting heavier and heavier as I approached Pen-y-Gwryd.

The grind up to the top of the Pass seemed interminable, and when I eventually got there it turned out that the cottages actually belonged to the hotel, which was beyond my means. So on I trudged down the Pass, hoping that I would be able to get bed and breakfast in Nant Peris. Somewhere around Dinas Cromlech, I emerged from the mist and spotted a little cottage to my left which, I later found out, was Cwm Glas Mawr cottage, a place I would become more and more attached to over the years. I knocked rather timidly at the door, which was opened by a tall man who seemed quite sympathetic when I explained what I wanted, and went to consult his wife. The couple were Mr and Mrs Powys and, for the week I was with them, they provided me with bed and board, and looked after me with every possible kindness – and all for 20 shillings!

Of everything that happened on that week's holiday, it is the view of Tryfan from The Glyders and my first rock climbs that I remember best. I was lucky to get the opportunity to climb at all as there weren't many rock climbers about in those days, but on the Wednesday two medical students passed the cottage bound for the popular climb called The Parson's Nose. When I asked if I could come along and watch they agreed without hesitation, and I must have impressed them with my enthusiasm on the way up because they then explained that they had two ropes and invited me to climb with them. We did The Parson's Nose and followed it with The Gambit Climb: I enjoyed every minute and every move. The Nose is an easy beginners' route with a certain amount of character, but The Gambit Climb is an absolute gem: plenty of exposure, a satisfying variety of moves, and one or two slabby bits which were not easy in the clinker-nailed boots that most of us wore in those days.

The week I spent with the Powyses was special in many ways, and the couple's generosity proved extraordinary when, later that year, I wrote to them asking whether there was any possibility of two of us – myself and a friend – staying with them over the coming Christmas. Their reply was brief: simply that they regretted that they would be unable to look after us as they had arranged to spend Christmas with their daughter in South Wales but that, if I wished, they would leave the key to the cottage at the post office in Nant Peris, where we could collect it and look after ourselves.

Christmas came, and my friend and I took up the Powyses kind offer. This time, we cycled over the Denbigh Moors to Snowdonia through the night, arriving at Betws-y-Coed in time for breakfast. The grind up to Capel Curig on the bikes was as exhausting as ever, but we quickly forgot how tired we were when we saw Moel Siabod covered in snow, and a heavy covering at that. In the early morning light, it was simply majestic. It was the first time either of us had seen snow on a mountain, and it was some time before we could turn our backs on this spectacular sight and get on our way again.

I won't dwell on the struggle we had pushing our bikes to the top of Pen-y-Pass – thankfully there was no camping gear to add to our heavy loads on this trip – but we got to the top eventually and were soon whizzing down the Llanberis Pass, hardly even noticing the crags on which I would be doing some of my hardest routes some 40 years later. By this time, we were anxious to get down to Nant Peris and collect the key to Cwm Glas Mawr cottage, and, after a quick breakfast, two very tired teenagers fell into bed. We had cycled nearly 100 miles, much of it across very hilly terrain, at night, and on heavily laden bikes.

After lunch, having slept through the rest of the morning, we decided that there was still time to fit in a short rock climb before it got dark. A little gully on the left of Dinas Mot, a crag in the Llanberis Pass, seemed to be just what we were looking for, but when we got there the rock was glazed with ice so I abseiled off after the first pitch – my very first abseil. This was just as well because we'd hardly started down the scree when a mass of ice came clattering down the gully. The following day, my friend decided that climbing icy rock was not his idea of fun and went off cycling, leaving me free to have a look at The Snowdon Horseshoe, which was in splendid winter condition.

The Horseshoe is a great expedition which combines a succession of outstanding views with a satisfyingly energetic day, and is as rewarding in its own way as anything I have done in the Alps, where the technical hazards can be similar. I can't remember exactly how many times I've completed the expedition – the last occasion was shortly after my eightieth birthday – but it's a considerable number. On one occasion, sometime after my retirement, I remember with some amusement being asked by two brothers to take them around it. The conditions were very misty and the boys lacked my familiarity with the terrain. The older of the two was studying physics and the younger divinity, with the intention of following his father into the Church, and when the latter expressed surprise that I was able to find my way around in the mist, I was half inclined to say that there may have been a bit of divine intervention, but I resisted the temptation to pull his leg. Safely back in camp, or rather the barn where we had spent the night, I made them a cup of tea before they set off on the unenviable task of hitch-hiking back home to Essex. As they left, the younger boy shook my hand and said, very earnestly, 'Thank you for a lovely day and for the tea and guidance'. I couldn't help feeling that he was well suited to his chosen profession.

In winter, The Horseshoe is a serious mountain excursion and that Christmas, as I neared the summit of Crib Goch, I became more and more apprehensive about tackling the Crib Goch Ridge on my own. Fortunately, there were a number of climbers on the summit, and so I followed a small group of them around The Horseshoe. It was a fortunate meeting on all counts because I got on so well with one of the members of the group, George Lewis, that before the day was out we had agreed to meet up for a week's climbing in the Lake District the following summer.

The following day, our brief holiday over, my friend and I set off on the long ride back to Lancashire. The weather forecast was poor and, in order to avoid the worst of it, we decided to go home by the coast road, which was quite a bit longer but less hilly. On our way through Llanberis, I bought a little picture of Snowdon. It was nothing special, but it caught my eye, and throughout the miserable journey home my main concern was to keep it dry. This was in the days before the universal plastic bag, and so I tucked the picture under my jumper – 'jersey' or 'pullover' in those days – to make sure it came to no harm and cycled on: 100 miles of dreary road, relentless rain and – to add to our misery – I got a puncture just five miles from home and had to leave my bike at a nearby house and finish the journey by bus. I did get the picture home intact though, which was fortunate because this marked the beginning of a love of landscape paintings, especially those in which mountains are a prominent feature, which has given me the greatest possible pleasure.

By Easter, I wanted to see more of the mountains in their wintry condition and, luckily, I found that my old school friend, Norman Rickard, was willing to join me, even though he had never done any mountain climbing in winter before. I had managed to buy an ice-axe for 30 shillings, but that was all we could afford, so we set off for the Lake District knowing that we would have to do a bit of improvising once we were on the snow slope. With only a limited knowledge of the area, I chose the gully on the east side of Bowfell Buttress, a very conspicuous gully in an attractive setting. The bike ride up to the Lake District was much less strenuous than our excursions into Wales, with far fewer hilly stretches, and we took our time going up Langdale before settling down for the night in the barn at Middlefell Farm.

I will always remember the view of Langdale the next morning. It is a magnificent valley at any time and, in my opinion, beyond compare in good snow conditions. Well lit from the east, it looked splendid, and the gully we were planning to climb appeared to be in perfect condition, although there was a pretty big cornice at the top. We were still wondering how we were going to manage without a second ice-axe – not that we were particularly worried as we were sure we would cope somehow – when we spotted a little fence post lying by the roadside, complete with sharp point, which we decided to use as a snow stake. Finding a rock suitable for hammering the stake into firm snow proved more of a challenge, but eventually we found what we needed and set off up the approach path to Bowfell.

The traverse across to the foot of the gully needed care as we had no crampons and were reliant on our clinker-nailed boots – but it did give me the opportunity to practice my step-cutting. As we climbed and got closer to our gully, it became apparent that the cornice was huge and that it would take some time to cut a way through it. We pitched the climb much as you pitch a rock climb. After running out a length of rope, I secured myself to my ice-axe, which was driven deep into the snow, then steadily took in the rope as Norman climbed

THE HEAD OF LANGDALE

For many walkers and climbers, their favourite corner of the Lakes, with miles of splendid hillwalking close at hand. Gimmer Crag, which has some of the best rock climbing in the UK, is just a little further up the valley.

up to join me. He then drove the wooden stake into the snow, and belayed to it, after which I carried on up the gully which, I seem to recall, is about 600 feet long. When we reached the cornice, we took it in turns to hack a way through and, four hours after we hammered in the first stake, we finished the climb – all a bit unorthodox, but it worked. We enjoyed ourselves immensely; in fact, we were so wound up that we broke the ice on a tarn nearby and had a dip, only to emerge freezing – perhaps not the best idea we had that day!

Some 40 years later, after my retirement, the same gully was the setting for a strange sequence of events that led to the local mountain rescue team being called out. It all happened as a consequence of a chance meeting with a climber who hitched a lift with me one day as I was driving up Langdale in search of some climbing myself. He mentioned that he had a couple of days to spare before he was due to join friends in Borrowdale, and that he was hoping to find someone to climb with in the meantime. I was in a similar position, so we agreed to team up for the day and, on arriving at the head of Langdale, decided to make for the gully on the east side of Bowfell Buttress.

In crampons – by now a standard piece of climbing equipment – the traverse across to the foot of the gully was straightforward enough, but we hadn't gone far when we spotted a long slide mark, obviously made by someone falling from the crags above and coming to a halt in a patch of soft snow. Here, there were traces of blood, but the unfortunate climber couldn't have been severely injured because a set of footprints led away down the snow slope towards the bottom of the valley and, as there was only one set of footprints, he had clearly managed to get down without help.

We were still wondering whether to turn back and report what we had seen to the mountain rescue team, when we heard a dog bark from somewhere high above, suggesting that there might be someone else up there, possibly in need of help. Cramponing up the slope above us was easy enough at first, but the slope soon got considerably steeper and it wasn't long before we were climbing on the two front points of our crampons.

My companion was the first to reach the dog, which was stuck all alone on the top of a small crag, feeling very sorry for itself. To my surprise, he shouted that he was going to try to get the animal off but, just then, he somehow lost his footing and came flying past me, eventually coming to a halt several hundred feet below, not far from where we had first seen the blood stains. In the course of the fall, he lost both his ice-axes, short axes which had proved totally inadequate when he used them to try to arrest his fall. Luckily, although obviously shaken and with a gash on his cheek where a flying ice-axe had caught him, he was soon sitting up and waving. I had always preferred the long axe, and it was with the greatest possible care that I now drove it into the snow as I made my descent.

Shortly after I got down, we were joined by two other climbers who had witnessed the accident from Bowfell Buttress, and together we shepherded my companion down to Middlefell Farm, where the mountain rescue team, which was based at the head of Langdale, was waiting. From there, he was taken to the local hospital where his injury was confirmed as a superficial gash and treated accordingly, while I had to give the mountain rescue people a full report of what had happened. They warned me that they had to report the accident to the local police and that an account might appear in the press, so I took some time drafting a careful statement. It seems that two reports did emerge in the end: one in the national press, briefly but accurately outlining what had happened; the other, I was told, in a local newspaper somewhere in the South of England, which apparently reported that my companion had been killed. As to the dog, I later learned that the mountain rescue team had sent two of their members up the mountain that night, but that the light failed before they could reach him. Luckily, they found him in good shape the following day, and were able to bring him down safely.

But all of this happened years after I first climbed the gully with Norman Rickard. That first Easter trip with Norman had shown us how much splendid climbing there was in the area, and I was looking forward to the following summer and the holiday in the Lake District that George Lewis and I had promised ourselves when we met doing The Snowdon Horseshoe the previous Christmas.

It was the summer of 1939, and George and I met at the railway station in Windermere about mid morning. Out of curiosity, I weighed my rucksack: 53 pounds. With a groundsheet that weighed as much as the tent, there was nothing light about climbing or camping gear in those days, and I certainly felt the weight of it as we began the long ascent up Rossett Ghyll. It seems that the Ghyll has always had a reputation in Lakeland folklore for its steepness because I remember a short verse that I came across many years ago, though I can't recall exactly where I read or heard it. It went something like this:

> If I were a lover who loved a lass,
>
> Who lived on top of Rossett Pass,
>
> I'd love her and cherish her for ever and ever,
>
> But go up to visit her, never oh never!
>
> (*Source unknown*)

The day was a scorcher, but in spite of the struggle we had with Rossett Ghyll, we arrived at Sty Head with enough energy to go on to climb Napes Needle by the classic route, followed by a brisk walk to the summit of Great Gable. It was a truly memorable day: the walk up the head of Langdale itself was a delight and, once we had the Ghyll behind us, the high-level path to Sty Head revealed the central hills in all their splendour.

We camped for the night on Sty Head and were up by six the next morning, which had all the makings of a lovely day. We certainly made the most of it because, by lunchtime, we had polished off Kern Knotts Crack, the Innominate Crack and the Sepulchre; classified as one 'severe' and two 'very severes', these were pretty hard routes by pre-war standards and neither George or I had attempted anything like them before. Naturally, we felt rather pleased with ourselves.

In the earliest days of mountaineering, the basic classification – 'easy', 'moderate' and 'difficult' – was sufficient but, as standards of climbing improved and climbers tackled more and more difficult routes, something more sophisticated was needed. By the time the war broke out in 1939, the grades ranged from 'easy', 'moderate', 'difficult' and 'very difficult' through to 'severe', 'very severe' and 'hard very severe'. Since then, improved climbing techniques and better equipment have led to climbs that are classified as various grades of 'extreme' or by a sophisticated numerical system. All an indication of the extent to which standards of climbing have gone up. It is worthwhile remembering, when comparing climbing grades from different times, that the only equipment the early climber had was a hemp rope of doubtful strength, a pair of nailed boots, and a pair of gym shoes, generally known as 'rubbers'.

George and I were to discover just how inadequate a hemp rope could be later that day on Kern Knotts Crack as, shortly after we finished the Sepulchre, a climber leading the Crack 'came off', as we climbers say, and the rope snapped on what was a comparatively short fall. These days, a climber attempting a hard route thinks nothing of coming off, protected as he is by a rope of phenomenal strength, his helmet, and an astonishing array of jamming devices designed specifically to arrest his fall; but I started climbing in the days when the rule was 'the leader doesn't fall', and I have always preferred to keep it that way. The astonishing thing about the fall we witnessed on the Crack was that, after falling 30 feet or so and landing on some very nasty rocks, the climber was able to get up and, after a short rest, make his way down to Borrowdale unaided.

That fall did, I must confess, shake our confidence though, and during the rest of the week we climbed nothing but fairly easy routes, although these did include some real gems, such as Moss Ghyll and the New West on

Pillar Rock. A few days after we had returned home, war broke out and George was called up into the Royal Air Force. I was to meet him just once more, at a service depot in Warrington, after which our paths diverged and we lost touch. It would be nice to think that he might read this account and make contact – he was a staunch companion and a great rock climber.

As it happened, it was on Sty Head, a year or so later, that I met and climbed with one of the Lake District's most celebrated characters. Millican Dalton, the self-proclaimed 'Professor of Adventure', was, I think it is fair to say, among the first to run a climbing school. I was carrying a rope and looking for someone to climb with when I was approached by an old gentleman dressed in a pair of cut-down trousers, no socks, and a broad-brimmed hat. Born in 1867, Millican Dalton rejected a conventional life at the age of 36, embracing instead the great outdoors and spending the rest of his life living under canvas, in shacks and, famously, in a cave in Borrowdale. That day on Sty Head, spotting my rope, he told me it was his 73rd birthday and that he would be most grateful if I would take him up the great Lakeland classic, Napes Needle. I knew nothing about his background or reputation at the time, but he climbed the Needle in fine style. From what he said, I gathered that he was living in the cave in Borrowdale at the time we met, and over the years I have come across a number of articles in the press about the man and his activities. I seem to remember being told that shortly after he quitted the cave, the roof fell in.

In the early months of 1944, the year I joined the army, I was lucky enough to fit in a number of short climbing trips, two of which were memorable for quite different reasons – one was quite funny, the other very frightening.

The first of these was when John Taylor, another old school friend, and I decided to have a look at Dow Crag near Coniston, a crag neither of us had climbed on before. On the first day, the weather was quite good and we did one or two routes, the names of which I can't remember, although I do remember thinking that they were somewhat more difficult than their grading implied. On the second day, it rained incessantly and so we pottered about in Coniston for a while before deciding to amble up The Old Man. By the time we had finished, we were soaked through and needed somewhere to dry off. Fortunately, on the way back to the tent, we came across a dilapidated old quarryman's hut on the flanks of The Old Man itself, with huge baulks of timber outside, all obviously abandoned for many years.

A quick forage around the hut provided us with enough kindling to start a fire, which we quickly stoked up into a welcome blaze, and the problem then was how to dry our clothes without scorching them. We solved the dilemma by draping our clothes over an arrangement of poles, suitably distant from the flames – or so we thought. We obviously hadn't got the arrangement quite right, however, because when John took his trousers – the only pair he possessed – down from the spar he'd hung them on, most of the seat fell off leaving a hole about a foot square. Again we foraged around in the hut, this time for something to patch the trousers with, and eventually found some dirty white canvas which we hacked into an appropriate shape with a pen knife.

The next job was to attach the patch to the trousers, so we punched holes in the canvas and in the trousers with a tent peg and crudely stitched the two together with a piece of string. The result looked decidedly odd, but it had to do – after all, there was no one about to see us. It was a different matter, though, when we arrived home and had to walk through busy streets on a Sunday night – we got some very funny looks indeed!

The second of the two trips was quite bizarre. This time, John and I were climbing at Ogwen in Snowdonia and thought we would have a look at Great Gully on Craig yr Ysfa, one of the best gully climbs in the UK. On the way back, we decided to take in Carnedd Dafydd and Pen yr Oleu Wen, and enjoy the view of Tryfan and The Glyders opposite. Coming down, we ran into thick mist but this didn't worry us as the descent to the lake, Llyn Ogwen, is straightforward.

But suddenly, as we emerged from the mist about 250 feet above the lake, we were frightened out of our wits by a series of bangs louder than anything we could have imagined, followed by the rattle of machine gun bullets hitting rock. With no time to think, we dived into a large cleft between two rocks, where we were probably safe enough – barring a direct hit – but it was very frightening, and it was probably the fear as much as anything that kept our heads down until all the noise had stopped. It was a while before I realized that we were in the middle of a field firing area and, worse still, on the wrong side of a creeping mortar barrage, a realisation which was confirmed when we heard the troops coming back down the hill.

It was a very odd experience indeed, but even stranger is the fact that, just over a year later, as a young officer cadet based at Penmaenmawr, I took part in exactly the same exercise as those troops – an assault crossing of Llyn Ogwen, using live ammunition, intended as a simulated crossing of the River Rhine. Fortunately, I was never called on to do the real thing.

THESE TWO SNAPSHOTS SHOW THE ASSAULT CROSSING OF LLYN OGWEN, IN WHICH A FRIEND AND I GOT CAUGHT BY CHANCE IN 1944

The troops are undergoing training, using live ammunition, and they are about to cross Llyn Ogwen in Snowdonia. The purpose of the exercise was to simulate the battle conditions which troops might experience during a crossing by Allied Forces of the River Rhine. I was involved twice. The first time was in 1944, when John Taylor and I were coming down the hill shown in mist in the first snapshot; we found ourselves at the receiving end of the creeping mortar barrage. The second time was when I did the exercise the right way round as a young officer cadet a year later; I must be somewhere in the second snapshot.

THE FAMOUS DEMO ROUTE
AT SENNEN IN CORNWALL

It is not quite as hard as it looks.

CHAPTER THREE

Army days

In 1944, I was called up. The three and a half years I spent in the army provided me with few opportunities for climbing, but I was lucky enough, after the customary preliminary training, to find myself in places that offered plenty of opportunities to sail. I was commissioned into a unit which I didn't even know existed – the Army's Navy or, more officially, The Royal Army Service Corps Fleet – and was posted to Rothesay on the Isle of Bute in Scotland for most of the autumn.

It was all I could have wished for as a posting: the location is a pleasant one and the work was interesting, learning the rudiments of navigation and ship handling on the lovely waters off the west coast of Scotland. There were a number of sailing dinghies at our disposal in our free time and, although I knew very little about boats initially and had never sailed before, I made good use of them, gradually becoming more confident in handling a dinghy in the blustery conditions so frequent that autumn.

One Saturday afternoon, however, I got rather more than I had bargained for when I took one of the dinghies out across the Clyde Estuary towards Wemyss Bay. During the outward journey the conditions were quite moderate and presented no difficulties, but on the way back the wind freshened considerably and a lumpy sea soon built up. The little boat needed careful handling for the last half hour or so, as I neared the Bute shore, and at one point I was steering with one hand and bailing with the other. But it didn't amount to any more than that and I never felt that the conditions were really dangerous.

Our colonel, who had told me off once before for sailing single-handed and had, apparently, been watching my progress through binoculars, appeared to think otherwise. On my arrival back at the mess, I was greeted by a very stern-looking commanding officer with the words, 'Dutton, I really don't know what to do with you: whether I should put you on a charge for needlessly hazarding one of the Army's dinghies, stop you sailing altogether, or buy you a drink.' When I replied that I would much prefer the drink, if he didn't mind, his mood changed, as I thought it might, and he beckoned me warmly over to the bar.

Occasionally, at weekends, I was invited – by some chaps I'd met in the harbour – to help crew a real ship, a lovely gaff-rigged cutter called *Coral*. At 28 feet, *Coral* was the biggest sailing boat I'd been on and on one occasion we sailed her around the Isle of Arran. This was the first time I'd sailed right round the island; it was a memorable trip and I had a feeling that one day I would return to Arran, which I did – in my own boat, *Vixen* – some 40 years later. Never for a moment, though, did I imagine that when I finally returned I would spend two whole summers cruising in those splendid waters.

The few weeks I had at Rothesay were among the most enjoyable of my army days. The Clyde and the nearby lochs provide some of the finest sailing in Britain; indeed, yachtsmen with a much wider experience than I have claim that it is some of the best in the world. Then, as the autumn drew to a close I was sent down to Bursledon, near Southampton, to learn more advanced navigation, where I was again fortunate, this time in being able to sail a classic little sailing cruiser called *Zenocrate*, made available to us in our free time. Far sooner than I would have wished, however, and quite to my surprise, I was posted to Cairo, but not before Phyl – a pretty, young physiotherapist, who I'd met in Woking – and I had become engaged.

Just as I was beginning to get used to Cairo – even here I managed to fit in some sailing, making the most of the sailing dinghies the army had available on the Nile to cool down in the hot afternoons – my unit was moved to the shores of the Great Bitter Lake, a sizeable stretch of water roughly in the middle of the Suez Canal. Here, too, most afternoons were spent swimming or sailing, as it became very hot after lunch and many units worked mornings and evenings. Dinghy racing was very popular and highly competitive, a little too competitive at times as I have never really been that way inclined. But, by luck or good judgement, I did manage to win the command championship racing a Snipe dinghy on one occasion!

After a year in Egypt, I was due 14 days home leave and Phyl and I took the opportunity to get married. It was in December 1946, and we headed off for a week's honeymoon in Cornwall, where we thought we might fit in some sailing on the Helford River. After our first day, when we did, as it happened, enjoy a lovely afternoon's sailing, we returned to the hotel only to find that I was required to report to the War Office in London the following day. The timing was hardly ideal and I had to spend the next two days in London, but the episode did have a positive side in that I was promoted and was told that I was to remain in the south of England for another ten weeks.

After a further spell of duty in the Canal Zone during which time our first son, Robert, was born, I was demobbed and rejoined my family. It was time now, I felt, to ease up on the climbing and find something we could do together as a family. As luck would have it, Phyl was very keen on sea fishing, having acquired a passion for the sport when, as a little girl, she was taken sea fishing off Bexhill by her grandfather, where they caught a lot of fish. As for young boys, most, given the chance, love fishing, and so our holidays steadily

PHYL ENJOYING HER KIND OF HOLIDAY

I think the fish is a tope, a small one by Phyl's standards. The highlight of these family holidays was the eight years we spent fishing off the west coast of Ireland, where this fish was caught.

became fishing holidays, in which the whole family – we had two boys by this time, Robert and Andrew – could take part. And so, apart from a quick trip north on my demob leave to visit my parents and have a look at Ben Nevis, my climbing days came to an end – for the time being.

The years I spent fishing for salmon and sea trout I have already described in another book (*Salmon and Sea Trout Fishing*; Faber & Faber, 1972), but there are some highlights from our family fishing holidays that are worth a mention. These holidays were mostly spent sea fishing, from a boat whenever we could manage it, and, looking back on some of those trips, I have often felt that we were more vulnerable fishing than I ever was sailing or climbing – it was always so difficult to get Phyl to pack up if the fish were biting! Over the years we had some very large catches indeed – and some very odd experiences, too – but, as so often happens, our largest fish got away. Looking back, this was probably just as well, as we would have had trouble getting some of them aboard!

There was the occasion in the early 1960s off the west coast of Ireland when Phyl hooked a skate which we realized was a big one when it began to tow the boat, a heavily built wooden craft about 16 feet long. This performance went on for a good half hour while Phyl slowly recovered line and worked the fish – whose weight the boatman estimated at over 200 pounds – to the surface. Neither he nor I fancied the idea of trying to lift the skate over the side as this risked capsizing the boat, but we thought that with two gaffs and a bit of luck we might just get it over the stern. Fortunately, perhaps, and to my relief, we were just reaching out with our gaffs when the fish dived, bringing the tip of Phyl's rod down on the gunwale with an almighty thwack, and the line broke.

During one holiday on the Welsh coast, Phyl and I stayed at St Davids in Cardigan Bay and spent a day as a local fisherman's first clients, fishing from a boat that had only been recently fitted out for rod fishing. We had a very good catch and an exciting quarter of an hour or so while Phyl struggled with a very lively fish, a tope which tipped the scales at 32 pounds. We tied its tail to the boom and I took a photograph, with the boatman standing on one side of the fish and Phyl on the other – quite an impressive picture as the tope was bigger than either of them. That night, we heard on the local news that a major fishing competition held at Tenby had been won with a tope of 26 pounds. Phyl felt very pleased with herself indeed and, sometime later, hoping to help the fisherman with his new business, I sent him a copy of the photograph, which, sadly, he didn't acknowledge.

Twenty years later, our son Andrew and his wife were on holiday at St Davids and, feeling like a day's sea fishing, they asked around about who might be willing to take them out. They were directed to a fisherman's cottage and the owner confirmed he could fit them in the following day. When Andrew asked what sort of fish he usually caught, the fisherman replied that if they would hang on for a minute he would show them. Disappearing into his kitchen, he returned with a photograph, which he handed to Andrew who promptly burst out laughing before explaining that the woman in the photograph was none other than Phyl, his mother! The fisherman was clearly a little embarrassed at this, as the photograph I had sent him all those years before was now getting somewhat dog-eared. Still, it was pretty obvious that he'd been showing it to prospective clients for the past twenty years, so I'd helped him with his business after all!

Of all our family fishing holidays, it is the eight we spent on the west coast of Ireland I remember best, and I still recall, very vividly, the sight of Phyl struggling with a huge pollack – so big that it dragged her to her knees – on a rocky peninsula not far from Killybegs. Then there was the time off Dingle when we had hired a boat for the day. When it was time to head back home, the engine wouldn't start and I had to take the carburettor to pieces while the sea got rougher by the minute. This is not what you want in a part of the world where the sea can blow up at any time and, in the end, Andrew and I rowed for an hour or so before, trying the engine again, I finally got the boat started.

They were memorable days but times change and, as the boys got older, they began to spend more time with their friends than on family holidays. It was about this time that Phyl and I began holidaying in North Wales, mainly fishing the coast to the south of Caernarfon. With all my earlier climbing and walking in North Wales it was, perhaps, not surprising that I started, now and then, to fit in a bit of hill walking, gradually widening my field to include the Lake District and Scotland. It was on a trip to the Lakes after my retirement that I bumped into members of an extraordinary group of climbers, the Sybarite Mountaineering Club – a meeting which prompted me to take up rock climbing again – and it is to the Sybarites, as they liked to call themselves, that I affectionately devote the next chapter.

BEN NEVIS IN WINTER
Climbers come from all over the world to scale the ice gullies.

MIKE PLINT, THE PRESIDENT OF THE SYBARITE MOUNTAINEERING CLUB, LEADING A ROUTE
ON A CRAG IN THE LAKE DISTRICT, GORDON HARRISON SECONDING

Mike founded the Sybarite Mountaineering Club for climbers who were getting on a bit and preferred
something more comfortable than the bivouac sack at the end of the day. We were comparative youngsters
when I took this picture, perhaps around 60 years of age. On the last climb Mike and I did together, our
combined age was 149 years.

CHAPTER FOUR
The Sybarite Mountaineering Club

The Sybarite Mountaineering Club surely deserves its place in climbing history. It was formed in around 1970 when Dr Mike Plint, a distinguished engineer tired of all the spartan stuff associated with mountaineering, said to his wife, 'It's time there was a club for the likes of me: chaps who have done the hard stuff of mountaineering and now deserve an easier day's climbing, a comfortable hotel as a base, and off the rocks in time for tea.' When his wife suggested that he started the club himself, Mike followed up the idea and outlined his aims in a notice he posted in one of the popular climbing magazines. He was swamped with enquiries and, a few months later, the club had its first meeting.

My involvement with the club was almost as extraordinary as the character of the club itself. Sometime during the war, in about 1943, I put up a new route – or what I believed was a new route – in Borrowdale in the Lake District, initially top-roping it and then pushing it up the following day. Apparently there was a possibility that part of it may have been put up by an earlier climber, but nonetheless my route was duly recorded in the Fell and Rock Climbing Club journal under 'Climbs Old and New'. I called the climb the 'Sybarite Route' because it was luxuriously accessible, barely yards from the path to the Bowder Stone, and so quite a change from the long walk in that was regarded as an integral part of rock climbing in those days, crucial for limbering up. The easy access was the only respect in which the route was 'sybaritic', however, as otherwise it was a very serious climb. When I took some friends from the Coventry Mountaineering Club to try it several years after I'd first put it up, not one of them was prepared to lead it, so we did it with the security of a top-rope. I remember how pleased I was when the strongest member of the party remarked, 'Heaven only knows how you managed to lead that in a pair of Woolworth's gym shoes!'

About 30 years later, when I happened to be in Borrowdale again, I thought it would be interesting to have another look at the route, on the off-chance that there might be climbers on it. As it turned out, there was no one about and so instead I decided to have a look at the popular route on Gillercombe Buttress, such an old favourite of mine that a friend and I once did it three times in an afternoon. On reaching the Buttress, I was surprised to find a party of elderly gents roping up at the foot of the crag. After a morning spent looking at the Sybarite Route, I had apparently stumbled across the Sybarite Mountaineering Club! We were soon exchanging experiences and when they learned that I had done some climbing in my younger days, they invited me to join them.

The Sybarites were a group of like-minded climbers, often hand-picked as members by Mike himself, who remained very much the driving force behind the club's aims and ideals, and planned and organised the formal meets, perhaps three or four of them a year. When I knew them, the Sybarites seemed to enjoy the climbing in Wales most of all, and regular meets tended to be based at the hotels in Betws-y-Coed or Capel Curig, although I do recall one or two very rewarding meets at Coniston in the Lake District. Then, once a year, there would be a dining meet in London or Oxford, to which our wives were also invited. Outside the formal meets, members also arranged excursions on a more casual basis which allowed for a good variety of trips. Several members of the club preferred to climb behind local guides, but a few of us liked to lead and it was my privilege, on one occasion, to take a party of Sybarites up a route in Gwynant Valley. Our combined age – there were three of us – was 201 years and the route was graded 'very severe': not bad for a group of elderly gents!

Even when the club ceased to have regular meetings, Mike Plint and I climbed together, and it was with Mike and Roger Baxter-Jones, a young English mountain guide working in Chamonix, that I first did any serious climbing in the Alps when we climbed Mont Blanc. On our last route together, when Mike and I climbed the Corner Buttress on Wintour's Leap, a popular rock climb in the Wye Valley, our combined age was 149 years.

For me, there is no doubt that the Sybarite Mountaineering Club deserves a place in mountaineering history, not only because its meets gave so much pleasure to its members but more especially because, over a period of 25 years or so, the Sybarites demonstrated that it was more than possible to carry on serious mountaineering well into what is popularly known as 'old age'. I will always look on that day on Gillercombe Buttress as one of the luckiest days of my life as I enjoyed the company of the Sybarites until its founder died and the Club gradually faded away.

THE VIEW OF MONT BLANC FROM THE AIGUILLES ROUGES

WALKING IN THE AUSTRIAN ALPS DURING A HOLIDAY ARRANGED BY THE RAMBLERS' ASSOCIATION

This was my first visit to the Alps and it left a deep impression. Little did I realise what it would lead to.

CHAPTER FIVE
Chamonix and Mont Blanc

Just before my retirement and shortly after I'd taken up hillwalking again, a friend who had done a lot of walking in the Alps suggested that I join him on a holiday in Austria arranged by The Ramblers' Association. The holiday was based on daily walks from Galtür involving some strenuous hillwalking and a little bit of quite serious scrambling. The weather was good and the mountain scenery very striking, and I enjoyed it so much that I had no hesitation, the following year, in joining him on another Ramblers' holiday – this time in the Stubai Alps, where we climbed a number of peaks, moving on from hut to hut most days. The Stubai is beautiful mountain country and the huts very comfortable and welcoming, just the kind of place to whet your appetite for more Alpine climbing.

And whet my appetite it did, as it was the following summer that I went to Chamonix with Mike Plint – my first trip to the Alps with fellow Sybarites – and, led by Roger Baxter-Jones, climbed Mont Blanc. I wasn't sure, at first, whether I particularly wanted to climb Mont Blanc, as a number of mountains near Chamonix looked more interesting, but its aura and its altitude – the mountain has an elevation of not much short of 16,000 feet – unquestionably had their appeal.

Mont Blanc dominates Chamonix in every sense of the word and, in fact, the town is often referred to as Chamonix Mont-Blanc. The mountain is not striking in itself in the way, for example, that the Matterhorn is, but the Mont Blanc Massif as seen from the Aiguilles Rouges on the opposite side of the Chamonix valley is undeniably one of the finest mountain panoramas in Europe: a huge wall of rock and ice, about 12,000 feet high. As a result, Chamonix derives much of its character from its proximity to and association with Mont

Blanc; a trifle brash and full of tourists in summer, it nevertheless steadily grows on you, and I can recall few visits of the many I've made to the Alps over the years when I haven't called in at Chamonix, or 'Cham' as climbers affectionately call it.

There are several routes up Mont Blanc which are climbed regularly and as many which are for experts only. We chose one of the easiest, taking the cable car from Les Houches and then making our way steadily up to the Tête Rousse Hut where the serious climbing begins. Shortly after the hut, the route crosses the Grand Couloir, a wide, ice-filled gully which acts as a huge rubbish chute. This is a gully you cross as quickly as you possibly can in order to avoid being swept away in the vast quantities of ice and rock that can come hurtling down at any moment. It is a major black spot on the mountain and, over the years, it has taken an inevitable toll in climbers' lives. Safely across the gully, you ascend steadily over steep rock and ice for something like 2,500 feet to the Goûter Hut, where the climb starts in earnest and where, if Mont Blanc is in anything like reasonable condition – with a good weather forecast and suitable snow – you can expect to find a lot of climbers.

The hut was packed when we arrived: the sleeping quarters we were allocated were so crowded that we had to lie on our sides in order to lie down at all and if, once down, you got up again, you had no hope at all of regaining your place. But that was over thirty years ago, and I understand that the accommodation has improved considerably since then.

The usual hour for leaving the Goûter Hut in those days was between two and three o'clock in the morning – so as to be able to get back down again before the sun started to soften the snow and risk of avalanche increased – so the climber was dependent on his head torch for quite some time. Dawn, when it does come – and it can seem an awfully long time coming when you are plodding along with only the glimmer of a head torch to light the way – can be a spectacle that quickly drives away the feeling that there are more sensible things to do than climb mountains, a feeling which all mountaineers must have experienced at one time or another. On a clear morning, the snowfields take on a rosy hue, which steadily intensifies as the sun rises to paint a scene of almost indescribable beauty.

From the Goûter Hut, the route is technically fairly straightforward, but you have to work your way up an extensive and very exposed snowfield and if bad weather moves in – as it can do with alarming rapidity in the Alps – the situation soon becomes very serious. Natural shelter is hard to find and for much of the route a crevasse may be the best you can hope for if you are to stay out of the wind and avoid hypothermia. Bad weather on this stretch of the route has cost many climbers their lives over the years and has forced some very strong parties to turn back. If there is time to reach it, the Vallot Hut can provide vital protection, but it is not a comfortable refuge. When Mike and I looked in on the way past, the hut was half filled with ice.

The long ridge from the Vallot Hut to the summit is easy enough in good conditions, but there are daunting drops on either side of you and in a wind of any strength you would be pinned down, unable to move, and facing the very real risk of being blown off. Rather surprisingly, despite having climbed in the Alps from the Savoy in France to the Dolomites in Italy, I have only once experienced a wind of menacing strength there,

HANG-GLIDERS ON THE SUMMIT OF MONT BLANC

The gliders were carried up the mountain and assembled on the summit. Hang-gliding seems a risky sport
even by mountaineering standards and a glider crashed while we were there. Fortunately, the pilot was able to
sort things out and was soon gliding gracefully down to Chamonix. At the time this photo was taken, gliders
were occasionally used to promote local trade and it wasn't unusual to see them soaring above Chamonix with
advertisements painted on their wings.

CLIMBING AT CHAMONIX

For French mountaineers, Chamonix is the centre of the mountaineering world and a lot of climbers would agree with them. Easily accessible from Geneva and half an hour from Italy – if you take the Mont Blanc Tunnel – it has the advantage of being at the foot of several of the highest mountains in the Alps. The climbers here are coming down from the summit of Mont Blanc. The hut below them is the Vallot Hut, an aluminium cabin which was half filled with ice when we were there. Nevertheless, its shelter has saved many lives over the years. The huge cracks ahead of the party are an indication of the state of the snowfield they are about to cross.

whereas in the UK – once on Ben Nevis and once on Moel Siabod in Snowdonia – I have been picked up by the wind and tossed 30 feet or more.

We found a surprising amount of activity on the summit of Mont Blanc when we got there, as a group of climbers had carried hang-gliders up the mountain and watching them assemble the gliders and take off was very interesting, though not something which I fancied trying myself. It seemed to me to be a risky game, even by mountaineering standards; indeed, one hang-glider crashed into the mountainside a few hundred feet below the summit while we were there, but the pilot was somehow able to sort himself out and take off again.

The view from the summit was naturally very extensive, but the surrounding hills looked dwarfed and were lacking much of their usual appeal. Hills, I find, generally look their best when seen from about mid-height. In spite of the view and the excitement of the hang-gliding, however, we didn't linger on the summit: it was about ten o'clock in the morning, the descent is a long one and we were hoping – in true sybaritic style – to get down to Chamonix in time for tea. We chose a different way down, a route which I seem to recall branched off from our ascent route shortly after we passed the Vallot Hut and then took us down past the Grands Mulets Hut.

At first, we made good time, which was just as well as there were stretches of the route which had obviously been swept by recent avalanches. Below the Grands Mulets Hut, however, our luck changed as the glacier became heavily crevassed and we seemed to spend hours trying to find a way off. By this time, it was obvious that we were going to be too late to catch the last cable car back down to Chamonix, so we decided to make the best of things and, finding a little café on the Plan de l'Aiguille still open, we dived in only to find that all they could offer us was a large plate of beans. It wasn't quite what we had hoped for, but we tucked in enthusiastically as we hadn't eaten anything substantial since leaving the Goûter Hut in the early hours.

We still had about 3,000 feet to descend before we reached Chamonix, but it was a lovely evening and the Aiguilles Rouges opposite Mont Blanc are a fine group of hills, so we took our time enjoying the scenery and that feeling of satisfaction that comes after climbing a major peak.

At Chamonix, however, I was in for a shock. Mike and Roger were both based in Chamonix, while I had planned to spend the night in Argentière, some four or five miles away. I took it for granted that by this time of night the last train to Argentière would have gone, as indeed it had, but was confident that I would get a taxi as it was only ten o'clock. But half an hour later, my searching and enquiries had still not produced a taxi and so I set off on the dreary plod. About half a mile from the village, a car stopped and the driver offered me a lift. He asked me where I'd come from and, as casually as I could and as if I always came down at about that time of night, I replied that I had just come down from the top of Mont Blanc. It was nearly one o'clock in the morning and I'd been on the go, practically non-stop, for 22 hours.

We spent the rest of our week's holiday rock climbing, starting with the classic route on the Aiguille de l'M, then moving on to a fine limestone crag above Cluses, where Roger was rash enough to whip a handkerchief out of a pocket that also contained a 100-franc note. We looked on in dismay as his hard-earned wealth fluttered gracefully down the crag, but Roger took it very philosophically, as if casting 100-franc notes to the wind was quite the natural thing to do. You can imagine our astonishment when, some time later, we were joined on the top of the crag by a party of Dutch climbers, one waving the errant note and enquiring, 'Whose is this?', claiming that it had simply floated into his hand as he reached up for a hold.

Although I enjoyed the ascent of Mont Blanc, perhaps more because of its atmosphere than its technical qualities, it was a climb that Roger and I did on the last day of our holiday, again on a limestone crag not far from Cluses, which I enjoyed most. It was an outstanding route. One of the early pitches was very hard, but the climb got easier after that, finishing up on a ridge made up of narrow ribs of rock which got fewer and fewer as we climbed, until we were climbing a single rib about four feet wide which soared up into the heavens. Roger later told me that we were the first British party to tackle the route.

The only other hard climb I have done on the Mont Blanc massif is the Couzy Route on the Aiguille de l'M, which I did with Geoff Watts and which was first climbed by Couzy and Prost in 1952. I remember that it took us about four hours – much longer than we expected – and recall one or two strenuous overhangs, but no outstanding difficulties.

Some of my most interesting climbs in the Chamonix area have been on the Aiguilles Rouges, the splendid range of hills immediately opposite Mont Blanc. It is a magnificent place to climb because, between pitches, you have the superb panorama of Mont Blanc laid out before you, surely the finest mountain vista in Europe. While the two popular routes on the Aiguilles Rouges – the Index and the Chapelle de la Glière – spring to mind, it was a little route called, I was told, the Voie de Désiré – though the climbers were far from sure that they had got the name right –which I remember best, because it was my last rock climb in the Alps. I was well into my seventies at the time. Of the other climbs – the Aiguille du Moine, the Aiguille du Tour, the Aiguille des Grands Charmoz – I remember the names, but few of the details.

I will always remember my first ascent of the Aiguille de L'M, however, because I spent the first night of my retirement stuck on the top. We were a party of four and we'd arranged that I should join the others as soon as I could get away from the office. It was shortly after midday when I arrived in Chamonix, and I was rather surprised when the only member of the party with any previous alpine experience suggested that we set off immediately for the Aiguille de L'M.

By the time we reached the foot of the climb it was late afternoon. The route is not long by alpine standards – about 600 feet, I seem to recall – but British climbers tend to be slow on alpine rock, having been brought up, as it were, on little crags where time is not as crucial, and we finished the last pitch just as the light was going. Fortunately, it was a fine night and we came to no harm, but bivouacking on a hard ledge on a rock pinnacle at something approaching 10,000 feet in the Alps is not everyone's idea of a comfortable retirement! The situation had its compensations however – in particular, watching the lights come on in the Chamonix Valley – and, after a while, I managed to snatch a little sleep.

The descent down the gully the next morning was straightforward enough, and we were soon back at the camp-site on the Plan de l'Aiguille, ravenously hungry. Fortunately, we had an ample supply of muesli which one of the lads had, apparently, bought in the Covent Garden Market at a knock-down price. We soon found out why it was so cheap: you could neither swallow the stuff nor spit it out and, once moistened, it was so

DESCENDING MONT BLANC

This is the heavily crevassed glacier which gave us so much trouble coming off Mont Blanc. It was one huge ice maze through which we steadily worked our way. The climbers are Roger Baxter-Jones, our guide, and Mike Plint.

OUR CAMP-SITE ABOVE CHAMONIX, WHERE I SPENT THE SECOND NIGHT OF MY RETIREMENT

The first night was spent on top of the Aiguille de l'M, one of the peaks behind Andrew Banks and Ray O'Neill, the two climbers by the tents. It was here that we had the trouble with the glutinous muesli that we simply couldn't swallow. I gather that camping is no longer allowed on this site.

SEEING THE ALPS THE EASY WAY

I took this photograph while lounging in a deck-chair on the sun terrace of a mountain restaurant above Argentière, a little village just north of Chamonix. I got there by cable car. This is one of dozens of outstanding viewpoints accessible by cable car in the Chamonix Valley and there are many other mountain centres in the Alps with similar facilities.

glutinous that the only way to get it out of your mouth was to scrape it out with a spoon. In the end, we presented it to a nearby colony of marmots and they were noticeably quieter for the rest of our stay. I have often wondered what they did about spoons.

Chamonix is a fine centre for walkers and climbers; in fact, it is just about the perfect Alpine venue. Even if the most you want to do is to sit and enjoy the spectacular scenery, Chamonix has it all: it is possible to reach the major view points by cable car, and where there is a cable car station there is usually a café or restaurant – ideal for those with sybaritic tendencies!

Some years ago, I was having a drink on the terrace of the café on the Brévent, when I saw all heads turn and an extremely pretty girl, accompanied by a tall, very distinguished-looking man, crossed the terrace into the café. The girl, I noticed, was wearing a very striking blouse which was, I thought, a little at odds with her climbing breeches and mountain boots. Her companion, I seem to recall, was wearing a kind of cape – not the apparel you would expect to see at something like 8,000 feet! They had just got off the cable car and I saw them only for a matter of seconds. I certainly never imagined I would encounter them again.

The drink finished, I decided to stretch my legs and ambled along the path to La Flégère with nothing particular in mind other than to get a bit of exercise and enjoy the view. But after a mile or so, I spotted an interesting crag about 400 feet down the hillside and I couldn't resist the temptation to go down and have a look. The way down wasn't all that easy, finishing up with a little gully and a lot of loose rock. On the crag itself, there was a party of Spanish climbers, obviously enjoying themselves.

Up to this point, I had no intention of climbing anything, as I was in my early seventies by now and doing less and less rock climbing. The climbs on the crag were short but looked quite hard. I watched the climbers for about an hour, getting more and more envious every minute, until I could no longer resist the temptation and went across and asked the leader of the party if there was any chance of being taken up one of the easier routes. I explained that I had neither climbing harness nor helmet, but that I had climbed in my younger days and would be happy to tie on with the rope around my waist, secured with a bowline, adding that this was standard practice when I started climbing. The Spaniards seemed to find this very amusing and one of them asked me, in excellent English, if I'd ever met Edward Whymper. My reply that I'd not only met him but had climbed with him on a number of occasions led to still more merriment, and one of the younger members of the party said that he would be pleased to take me up a route. In modern rock climbing footwear such as the Spanish climbers had on the route wouldn't have been too demanding, but in ordinary walking boots I found it quite hard.

Just as we were finishing the climb, there was a clatter of rock in the gully at the side of the crag and, shortly afterwards, the girl who had attracted so much attention in the café on the Brévent appeared, followed some time later by her companion. While he clearly wasn't at home on loose rock, the girl moved over the rough ground at the foot of the crag with all the confidence of someone thoroughly at home in the hills.

When I had finished the climb and returned to my rucksack, which I'd left on a nearby rock, the couple joined me and the girl, who was Italian but spoke English reasonably well, began to question me about the climbing

THE NANTILLONS GLACIER IN THE MONT BLANC MASSIF NEAR CHAMONIX

This is the approach route to a number of the most popular climbs in the Alps and the photograph illustrates all too clearly some of its hazards. It shows something like 4,000 feet of ice, masses of which are liable to come hurtling down at any time without notice, as glaciers on a slope are always on the move.

I'd done, but in a guarded sort of way. Later on, when her companion went across to talk to the Spaniards, she began to talk more freely, and it was soon obvious that she knew more about the climbing on the Aiguilles Rouges than I did. All the time she was talking, she was watching the climbers' moves carefully and I got the impression that she was itching to be on that crag. After a while, I left them, intrigued by what I'd seen and wondering how on earth she was going to get her companion back up that gully, but she obviously did because I saw them again two days later in Chamonix, a striking but rather oddly matched couple.

It would be easy to fill a book with details of the walks around Chamonix, and several people have already done so. There is, however, one mountain walk – or 'trek' as it is now called – which deserves more than a casual reference because it must surely be the finest mountain trek in Europe and that is the Tour du Mont Blanc. This is a trek around the Mont Blanc Massif which takes several days and entails a lot of serious walking, long ascents and descents, always with the possibility of bad weather catching you out when shelter is far away. It is important, therefore, that anyone doing the Tour is an experienced hill walker, well equipped and reasonably fit.

How long the Tour takes depends on the inclination and fitness of the party and the precise route you take, as there are alternative routes on some stretches, some of which may not be open early in the season. But this is not a guidebook and, since there are already some excellent ones available, both in English and in French, I will content myself with describing some of the highlights of the trip, which took me five days. Five days is quicker than I would recommend, but it was all I had left of a month in the Alps with Roger-Baxter Jones and Brian Shaw, when we climbed a number of major peaks and when I was pretty fit.

I began the tour at the Brévent and headed for Les Houches, enjoying the descending traverse which is dominated by the view of the Aiguille du Midi and the Aiguille de Bionnassay opposite. I remember little of the slog up from Les Houches to Bellevue other than thinking that it might have been more sensible to have taken the cable car, but that would have been cheating. It was beginning to get dark when I arrived at Bellevue, and I was soon snug in my bivouac sack on the hillside. For some strange reason, I had always had some reservations about spending part of a holiday walking around the Mont Blanc Massif, but what I had seen during the day and the view – in particular the views of Mont Blanc opposite and of the Chamonix Valley – which greeted me when I woke up the next morning quickly dispelled any misgivings I had, and so it was throughout the trip.

The following day, which took me through Les Contamines and up to the Refuge du Col de la Croix du Bonhomme, was less exciting scenically, but there was plenty of variety and I was pleased to see Les Contamines again as I had stayed there years previously with some friends from the North London Mountaineering Club, when we climbed the Aiguille de la Bérangère. After a meal in the hut, I took to my bivy sack again, thankful that I didn't have to sleep in the hut itself, which was very crowded. I had seen enough of alpine huts by this time to know that they are no fun when they are crowded, airless in many cases due to a reluctance to open windows even on the calmest of nights, and noisy with snoring in a dozen different languages.

DOING THE TOUR DU MONT BLANC ON BICYCLES

I met a couple as they made their way around the Tour du Mont Blanc on bicycles! Some days they must have pushed or carried their bikes up the best part of 3,000 feet. They were probably at about 8,000 feet when I took this photograph. The snowy summit of Mont Blanc can be seen behind the pinnacles.

I was up and away early the next morning. Shortly after leaving the hut, the country opened out again, with striking limestone peaks dotted amongst the snow and granite. The country from here on was new to me, and I was enjoying trying to identify the peaks around me when two cyclists came riding down the path and stopped as I stepped to one side to let them pass. You can imagine my astonishment when I discovered that they were a middle-aged English couple who had done the Tour du Mont Blanc on foot in their younger days and, having taken up cycling later in life, had decided to repeat the trip, this time on bikes! They were now nearly 8,000 feet above sea level, miles from anywhere, and on the previous day alone they must have pushed or carried their bikes uphill for the best part of 3,000 feet. But it was obvious that they were coping and now, with miles of downhill run before them, they were greatly looking forward to the ride ahead.

The next stretch downhill was easy, as I recall, but I was in no hurry as it was impressive country and I was now seeing Mont Blanc from a different angle, with great snowfields dominating the scene. After passing through Les Chapieux and crossing the Col de la Seigne, the scenery seemed to get more savage and rockier. At a distance, the upper snowfields of a mountain can often seem picturesque and almost benign, but this is a completely false impression, of course, as snow and ice are even more unstable than rock.

By the time I neared the Elisabetta Refuge, the day was getting very hot indeed and I was wondering whether to go up to the hut for a drink when I came to a little stall selling various refreshments, including bottled beer. It was a strange assortment, none of which I had ever seen before, but whatever the bottle contained, it tasted like nectar.

Of the rest of the way down to Courmayeur, I remember very little. It had been a long day, which got hotter and hotter as it went on, and my only concern was to find a little hotel and have a meal and a bath. I had spent most nights of the previous month in a bivy sack, and was beginning to get a little tired of the Spartan life; as a fully paid-up member of the Sybarite Mountaineering Club, I felt that I was entitled to a comfortable bed and a bath.

Courmayeur is a handsome little town, but I didn't linger when I passed through it the following morning as I was keen to see the next stretch of the tour, which is dominated by the Grandes Jorasses. Again, my general impression was one of savage, rocky lower slopes, liable to avalanche at any time. Indeed, here and there were signs of recent rockfalls which had reached right down to the road.

On the climb out of the Italian Val Ferret up to the Col Ferret, I was struck by the extent to which the lower slopes of the glaciers had shrunk. This shrinkage is having a dramatic effect on the Alps which, if it persists, will surely reduce their appeal: what were once smooth snow slopes, which reflected the light in a dozen different shades, are now often shattered ice-fields, which look intimidating and really offer little to please the eye. On the lower slopes, fine snow fields have vanished to reveal seemingly endless masses of rock rubble. For the mountaineer, this change is steadily making many of the routes considerably harder as the smooth slopes of firm névé, ideal for cramponing, give way to broken slopes of raw ice. What is causing this is a matter of conjecture; while Alpine glaciers have both retreated and advanced over the centuries, what now appears beyond doubt is that, as far as records show, the rapid rate of the current shrinkage is unprecedented.

I spent the next night in a bunk-house near La Fouly, whose only other occupants were two Dutch girls doing the Tour the other way around. They seemed to be enjoying themselves, but complained that there was nothing to do in the evenings. I don't think they particularly appreciated my suggestion that they could always go for a walk!

On my way the next morning, I passed the Amone Slab, an awe-inspiring piece of smooth rock over 1,200 feet high. I understand from friends who have climbed on the Slab that the main route is hard, but not desperate. I have always enjoyed slab climbing, where balance and footwork matter more than strength, and I made up my mind to fit it in one day but, unfortunately, I never did.

Champex, which was the next place I came to, was as pretty as the guidebook said it would be, but somehow or other it seemed a bit out of place after the wild grandeur of the country I'd just passed through. I spent that night in my bivy sack at Bovine, splendidly situated but, as the name suggests, with rather too many cows. I can still recall the smell!

After Champex, I was back in familiar country and remember little of the day until I reached Le Tour, a place I won't forget in a hurry as it wasn't far away that, some years earlier, I got into trouble coming down from the Albert Premier Hut. Richard Dees, another Sybarite, and I had climbed the Aiguille du Tour and, rather than spend the night in the Hut, I had decided to head for Le Tour and bivouac on the way down. The normal way from the Hut, as I remember it, follows a lateral moraine for some distance and then breaks away to easy ground on the right. On the descent, I was lost in thought and generally day-dreaming, and I forgot to quit the moraine when I should have done. Rather than go all the way back up again, I decided to carry on as the ground ahead seemed straightforward enough, mainly grassy slopes, albeit rather steep ones. But, as I descended, the slopes got steeper and steeper until it was clear that I was unlikely to find anywhere to lie down unless I had something to tie on to. This, fortunately, was no great problem as I had my ice-axe to hand, and I soon found a stone and drove the axe into the turf. Then, slipping on my climbing harness and attaching a sling, I clipped on to the axe.

I won't pretend that it was the most comfortable night I have ever spent, but dawn came at last and I set off down the hill, eventually arriving at a line of rocks. By now, I had picked up the faint signs of a track through the rocks but as the rock wall steepened I lost sight of the track and soon found myself climbing down the rock itself. This was a lot more difficult than I had bargained for, and I was soon drawing on those strange reserves which climbers seem to find on such occasions. Perhaps I should have turned back but, taking great care, I climbed steadily down and finally arrived at the foot of the crag in one piece.

Once back on familiar ground at Le Tour, I somehow felt that my Tour du Mont Blanc was over; it had been a splendid excursion and one I will always recall with pleasure. I was tempted to carry on across the Aiguilles Rouges, but I knew the Aiguilles Rouges well and time was now running out so I took the bus from Le Tour back to Chamonix.

GLACIER SHRINKAGE IN THE MONT BLANC MASSIF

This photograph was taken on the Tour du Mont Blanc and the size of the lateral moraine gives a clear indication of the extent to which the glacier has shrunk.

A SCENIC WALK ABOVE ZERMATT IN SWITZERLAND

The architecture of the lovely chapel reflects the outline of the shapely peak opposite. There is any amount of
attractive, high-level walking above Zermatt, one of the principle Alpine resorts dominated, of course,
by the Matterhorn.

CHAPTER SIX

Zermatt and the Matterhorn

When I'm in Chamonix, I'm always very much aware of the fact that I'm in France and that Mont Blanc is a French mountain. It's almost as if we climb on Mont Blanc by the kind permission of the French, which I suppose we do in a way.

In Zermatt, on the other hand, the feeling is totally different, almost as if the British had a kind of proprietorial interest in the place. I've heard other climbers express a similar sentiment. A few years ago, two elderly climbers, Mike Plint and I – looking, I suspect, as if we were closer to Edward Whymper's generation than to the mountaineers of today – were stopped in the main street of Zermatt and asked if there was a climbing museum in the town. Mike's reply – 'Yes, we're part of it!' – may have been intended to be nothing more than flippant, but I suspect that it reflected a little of the feeling of belonging to which I have just referred. As far as I can recall, the British were not notably involved in the early attempts to climb Mont Blanc, whereas they were deeply involved in the struggle to climb the Matterhorn, at first largely from the Italian side. The tragic accident which befell Whymper's party as they descended from the first successful ascent of the mountain – by the Swiss (Hörnli) Ridge from Zermatt – killing Swiss and British climbers alike, must surely have brought the two nations a little closer together.

Seen from Zermatt, the Matterhorn is a mountain of unmatched beauty. Furthermore, to see the Matterhorn from above Zermatt is, in my experience, the most striking angle of all. Its shape, its position, its unrealness – seen in some lights – have all served to make it universally admired, but as a climber you need to treat the Matterhorn with respect as its beauty hides risks that might all too easily prove fatal. Almost as if to illustrate the point, when we climbed the Matterhorn, the walls of the Hörnli Hut were adorned with battered climbing helmets, a warning of the dangers of rockfall, and on the summit ridge, on a day when I was assured that the weather was as good as one could possibly hope for, the rope, held up by the wind, billowed out sideways rather than hanging limp at my side. It is not hard to imagine what the conditions on the Ridge can be like in bad weather. In fact, an unexpected patch of bad weather scuppered our first attempt to climb the mountain and the unexpected blizzard caught out our friends who were pinned down for almost two days in the Solvay Hut, a small shelter about halfway up the Hörnli Ridge.

After climbing together for some time in Chamonix, a small group of us from the North London Mountaineering Club agreed to split up, with one party tackling the traverse of the Matterhorn from the Italian side, and the other – of which I was a member – going on to do the straightforward climb up and down the Hörnli Ridge from Zermatt. We were the lucky ones as it turned out as, quite by chance, we got a late weather forecast which announced that some unexpected bad weather was due to move in. Unfortunately, our friends in the other party, poised to make the ascent from Breuil-Cervinia on the Italian side of the Matterhorn, missed the forecast and climbed up to the Carrel Hut on the Italian Ridge, where they spent the night.

The weather the next morning was doubtful, but they were keen to complete the traverse of the Matterhorn and, after some hesitation, they decided to push on to the summit, which they reached after a struggle. They then set off down the Hörnli Ridge towards Zermatt. Conditions on the Hörnli Ridge were worse than anything they had had to cope with so far, but eventually they managed to reach the Solvay Hut. Here, they were stuck, together with a number of other climbers, for almost two days, until a particularly strong party forced a way down and they were able to follow. Meanwhile, a very anxious wife drove from one side of the mountain to the other – a distance of about 140 miles – several times, trying to discover what had happened to her husband.

A week later, with a promising weather forecast to reassure us, Brian Shaw and I, led by Roger Baxter-Jones, decided to have another go at the Matterhorn, again by the Hörnli Ridge from Zermatt. Roger advised us to get to the Hörnli Hut as soon as possible as the longer we spent at the higher altitude, the better we would cope the next day. I have never had any trouble with the altitude in the Alps, but it can affect some climbers badly, the reduced levels of oxygen causing breathing problems and debilitating fatigue. Somewhat to my surprise, Roger also asked us not to take any food other than snacks to eat on the way, explaining that he would bring food up with him to cook in the Hut and adding that we could expect him at about half past six.

We took Roger's advice and set off for the Hörnli Hut about mid-morning. The climb up to the Hut is straightforward and well-defined, as the path carries a lot of traffic in the summer months. As you climb, the view steadily becomes more open and impressive. We arrived at the Hut mid-afternoon to find it busy, but not crowded, and were surprised, given the fine conditions, to find that we were the only English party there.

Sitting around in huts, or on the terraces which usually surround the larger huts, is not my idea of fun, however spectacular the view, and as time went by we began to feel decidedly hungry. But half past six arrived

A PARTY JUST BEGINNING THE DESCENT OF THE MATTERHORN

ROGER BAXTER-JONES AT THE START OF THE ICE WALL
ON THE TRIFTJIGRAT ROUTE ON THE BREITHORN, NEAR
ZERMATT IN SWITZERLAND

When we did it, the ice wall was roughly 200 feet high and pitched at an
angle of about 70 degrees, the climax of a very serious route nearly 4,000
feet long. It was at this point that the helicopter came in close to see how
we were getting on.

and still no sign of Roger. By now, it was starting to get rather chilly on the terrace and so we moved into the Hut, where they were beginning to serve supper. Soon, we were the only people not eating, which was a bit embarrassing because, from the occasional glances we got, it was clear that the other climbers were beginning to think that we were the poor old English who simply couldn't afford to eat.

It was a quarter to eight when Roger arrived and by this time the diners had finished their rather frugal meals. An imposing figure, Roger immediately caught the attention of the assembled company, particularly when one of the most respected of the Zermatt guides rose from his seat and embraced him warmly. This was followed by some animated chat and much laughter and, by the time Roger came across to Brian and I, who had been watching the performance from a table in the corner of the hut, it was clear that no one knew what to make of it all. After greeting us like old friends, Roger unpacked his rucksack, taking out two Calor gas stoves, which he set up on the table, and a considerable quantity of food. Then, over the next hour, he proceeded to cook a four-course meal, which any restaurant would have been proud of. The other climbers looked on with obvious puzzlement and, I'm sure, not a little envy.

The Hörnli Hut is situated at about 10,500 feet and, once there, you still have something like 4,000 feet to go before you reach the summit of the Matterhorn. The customary starting time for this ascent seems to be about three o'clock in the morning, and the climbing starts immediately you leave the Hut, so for quite some time you are climbing by the light of your head torch. Fortunately, the climbing is not too difficult, but the rope handling needs careful attention and, with so much loose rock about, you have to take care not to knock rocks down on the heads of climbers below. By the time dawn breaks and you are able to switch off your head torch, you are beginning to move more easily and, indeed, to climb more quickly. The route is a long one and you are always aware that the weather can change dramatically and with little warning. Very experienced climbers have died of exposure within yards of the Solvay Hut, which we were soon to pass, pinned down by storms which make any movement on the mountain quite impossible.

As you ascend, the climbing tends to get more interesting, especially when you reach the fixed ropes. If there are a lot of climbers on the mountain, climbing this section can lead to problems, as there are times when climbers are going up and down the same rope at the same time. When I was halfway up one of the ropes, for example, a climber coming down managed to stick one of the spikes of his crampons inside my boot, which certainly didn't make things any easier.

Just when you are beginning to think that you will never reach the top, the Ridge levels out and you're there. On the summit of the Matterhorn – and what a feeling it is! – I was surprised by just how little time most climbers spent there, but I suppose this is to be expected. The view is superb, but at the back of your mind is the realisation that you are never safe until you are off the mountain. I can recall little of the descent apart from an acute awareness of the need for care, and the view of the Ridge – endless, it seemed – and Zermatt, snug in the valley below.

A few days later, we did the hardest route of the holiday and quite the hardest snow and ice route that I have ever done or ever wished to do: the Triftjigrat route on the Breithorn. The climb was entirely over snow and ice, and from the hut to the summit must have been nearly 4,000 feet. The most serious sections were the 200-foot ice wall, with its angle of nearly 70 degrees, and the exposed passage across an ice-field at the top of which were huge seracs which crashed down when they had tilted enough for gravity to set them moving. The ice wall was a serious test of our cramponing technique as we were on the front points of our crampons for the whole of the time we were on it. It was the sort of situation which gives climbers a sense of achievement but I can't say I enjoyed it. Roger and Brian were clearly in their element, however; at least, they were until a helicopter appeared on the scene and buzzed us from a matter of feet away, or so it seemed at the time. The huts in that part of the Alps are largely serviced by helicopter and we assumed at the time that they were buzzing us out of curiosity, but we were later told that climbers occasionally get into difficulty on the ice wall and are glad to be airlifted off in spite of the hefty fee.

Brian was now at the end of his holiday and set off for home early the next day, while Roger and I spent the day in Zermatt, planning to return to Chamonix in the evening. Unsure whether we would get a connection at Martigny, Roger thought he would try to hitchhike, but I decided to take the train only to find, on arriving at Martigny, that the last train to Chamonix had already departed. At first, I thought I would look for a hotel but, on coming to a road junction, I spotted the signpost for Chamonix and decided to try hitching after all. I had hardly turned to face the on-coming traffic when a car stopped and Roger waved me in. Apparently, he had spotted me as they came down the road and, fortunately, had been able to persuade the driver to stop and pick me up too.

I have visited Zermatt many times in recent years, just for the pleasure of seeing the place again. Wandering down the main street on my most recent trip, I happened to notice in one of the bookshops a striking print of the Matterhorn, which turned out to be a reproduction of a painting by the English painter Edward Theodore Compton (1849–1921). When I expressed an interest in the print, I was shown a large book containing over 100 early prints of the Matterhorn, including the one I had seen in the shop window and several others by Compton. A few days later, browsing through the art books in the library at Chamonix, I came across another book on mountain paintings published, if I remember correctly, by the Museum at Grenoble and here again the work of Compton was well represented. But most interesting of all is a book by Jürgen and Sibylle Brandes, published as recently as 2007 (Bergverlag Rother), entitled, simply, *E. T. Compton* and devoted entirely to the work of that artist. The book itself is a splendid piece of publishing running to well over 300 pages, most of them with fine, full-page, colour reproductions of Compton's mountain paintings.

Compton died in 1921 and his work has always been highly regarded, particularly in Europe, which is not surprising, perhaps, since he spent most of his life there and the majority of his paintings depict Alpine scenes. The appeal which mountains hold for British painters is perhaps deeper than one might expect, but it is undoubtedly there; indeed, one might say that it all started with Turner and Ruskin. Clearly, the appeal continues to exert its influence, as fine studies of mountains reach the galleries regularly, especially from painters in North Wales. Of these, the undoubted master is David Woodford, whose portrayal of the subtle lighting and atmosphere found in the hills of North Wales has never been matched, perhaps because few have cared to look so closely or are prepared to hone their skills to the extent needed to portray what they have seen on canvas.

THE PARTY BEHIND US ON THE MÖNCH

ROGER BAXTER-JONES (RIGHT) AND I IN THE CAVE WHERE WE BIVOUACKED BEFORE
BRIAN SHAW, ROGER AND I CLIMBED THE EIGER

CHAPTER SEVEN
The Eiger, the Mönch and the Jungfrau

On my first visit to the Bernese Oberland, I had the good fortune to be able to climb both the Mönch and the Jungfrau, two very enjoyable climbs and, by the popular routes which we took, not too difficult. When we reached the top of the Mönch, which involved cramponing up a narrow ridge, we were the only people there; by contrast, what I remember most about the Jungfrau is the number of climbers there were on the summit and the way in which much of the route is menaced by huge ice cornices. Grindelwald gets a lot of snow, and collapsing cornices are a major hazard on the mountain. Apart from this, my only lasting recollection is that I was slack in applying the sun-cream and was badly burnt, so much so that, in the customary summit photograph, I am hardly recognisable!

But you cannot spend long in Grindelwald without coming under the spell of the Eiger and, the following year, Roger, Brian and I made our way to a little cave at the start of the West Flank route. I was not particularly happy with the place because, as a true Sybarite, I can think of better ways of spending a night than in a damp cave, three-quarters of the way up the Eiger! To add to our discomfort, there was a strange, brooding atmosphere about the place and we soon had the feeling that we shouldn't be there at all. This disconcerting feeling certainly wasn't helped when two members of the local gendarmerie arrived, explained that a couple of climbers had left for the summit two days previously and hadn't returned, and asked if we would keep an eye out for them.

After an uncomfortable night which seemed interminable – I must confess that I was feeling distinctly apprehensive in a way I had rarely experienced before – we left for the summit. I don't recall any particular difficulties on the way up, apart from the awareness that, on much of the ground, a slip would be difficult to check and that on the few rocky bits which we encountered everything seemed to slope the wrong way.

Just after we had reached the summit and begun the descent, we sensed that the weather was beginning to change and shortly afterwards the condensation on our waterproof clothing began to freeze. Then the wind got up in violent bursts and it was soon obvious that we would need to move quickly if we were to get off the mountain alive. It was then that Roger's experience became invaluable and over the next two hours we were to learn what bad weather on the Eiger can be like, as he carefully shepherded us down the mountain. As we descended, the problem of the freezing condensation worsened: my cagoule became plated with ice the best part of an inch thick, which I shook off whenever I could manage to dislodge it, and the drawcord on its hood was transformed into a string of ice beads, each as large as a hazelnut. Fortunately, as we lost height, the ice gradually melted and, by the time we reached the cave where we had spent the night, the storm had blown itself out.

When we spoke to climbers in Grindelwald about the storm, they were clearly puzzled. They had been aware that something was happening on the summit of the Eiger, where vicious storms frequently envelop the mountain, but it had never occurred to them that on this occasion anything particularly menacing had happened.

I have been up to the cave where we spent the night only once since then, when I accompanied some friends on a sightseeing excursion. It was a beautiful day when we arrived but within half an hour clouds started to gather round the summit of the Eiger and soon enveloped the whole mountain. A few minutes later, a helicopter took off and began to search the West Flank route, apparently looking for two French climbers who had left for the summit that morning. Luckily, they were quickly spotted and airlifted off – only just in time, as it happened, as the storm raged for the next two days. Our little epic happened on the easiest route up the Eiger; I will leave you to imagine what a storm on the notorious North Wall must be like.

Having climbed several of the highest mountains in the Alps, I began to feel that I had done all I wanted to of the classic routes, with their long days and early starts. So, when Roger suggested that I try leading some of the less demanding mountains in the Italian Alps, I was happy to take his advice. On my first trip, with friends, we climbed the Gran Paradiso and La Tresenta from a hut above Pont and these, I felt, were the mountains of old age: easy climbing, reasonable starts, and weather markedly better than that in the main Alpine resorts.

My next excursion was to the Écrins where we climbed Pic Coolidge and a number of other peaks. It was here, at Ailefroide, that I learned that Roger, whom I had been due to visit in Chamonix on the way home, had been killed by an ice-fall while leading a hard route on Mont Blanc. It was sad news. Although there was a great difference in our ages, we had grown very fond of one another over the few years we climbed together.

AN ICE WALL ON THE
JUNGFRAU
Making the best of my
retirement. A bit off the
'ordinary route' this time.

APPROACHING THE SUMMIT OF THE JUNGFRAU

By the route we took, the Jungfrau is fairly straightforward in reasonable conditions, but it doesn't require much imagination to appreciate how serious the situation could become if the weather changed. The Jungfrau, the Mönch and the Eiger are all quite close to one another in the Bernese Oberland of Switzerland, for which Grindelwald is the accepted centre. They are amongst the most sought-after mountains in the Alps. Grindelwald is also a favourite centre for hillwalkers, with miles of well-used track.

CLIMBERS HALFWAY UP THE JUNGFRAU IN THE BERNESE OBERLAND

The mountains in this part of Switzerland have some of the
heaviest snowfalls of any mountains in the Alps and the
weather is some of the most fickle. The Eiger is only a few miles
from the Jungfrau. Even on the easiest routes it is impossible
to completely eliminate the risk of being overwhelmed by an
avalanche, as is very evident in this photograph.

A PARTY APPROACHING THE SUMMIT OF THE GRAN PARADISO BY
THE POPULAR ROUTE FROM THE RIFUGIO VITTORIO EMANUELE

The climbers are at about 13,000 feet. On the two occasions I've climbed
the Gran Paradiso, the ascent, by alpine standards, was straightforward;
nevertheless, care was needed on the summit rocks, which were glazed with
ice in places.

CHAPTER EIGHT

Further afield: mainly the Italian Alps

Andy Heald and I first met on the camp-site at Sligachan on the Isle of Skye, when we helped to push-start a car. We soon found that we had similar ideas about the climbs we would like to do and the next day we joined a party who were planning to climb the Great Prow on Blaven. The Prow is a classic Scottish rock climb, the best part of 400 feet long and graded 'very severe'. The climbing was interesting – with enough exposure and a good variety of moves – and not too hard, though there was the odd bit of loose rock which needed watching, as I discovered when a piece came flying down and struck my helmet. It wasn't particularly large – about the size of an egg perhaps – but it took a chip out of my helmet, and would certainly have taken a good chip out of my head had I not had the helmet on!

After one or two more climbs together, Andy and I agreed to spend a fortnight climbing in the Alps the following summer. We were especially lucky with the weather, which was perfect throughout the trip, and we saw a great deal of the Alps and packed in a lot of climbing. Our first night was spent high above Pralognan la Vanoise, poised to do the traverse of the Aiguille de la Vanoise the next day. It was an area quite new to us and we enjoyed the walk up to a little lake, where we camped.

We were just thinking of getting into our sleeping bags when, in the distance, we saw a group of people coming along the path. As they drew closer, we were astonished to find that there were at least twenty of them, some of them women wearing cotton frocks and clutching sleeping bags – not quite what you would expect to see at something like 8,000 feet and at nine o'clock in the evening! They turned out to be an Italian party, heading for the Felix Faure Hut. Apparently, they had heard how attractive the Vanoise is, and were determined to see it for themselves. They still had some way to go to reach the Hut, but they must have managed as we met them there the next morning and they seemed to be thoroughly enjoying themselves.

I have always been surprised by the intrepid nature of some of the Italian parties you meet in the Alps. I am not thinking of the hardened climbing fraternity, but of the hosts of Italians who pour out of the cities, especially at weekends, for a couple of days in the mountains. Perhaps the most astonishing example of this adventurous spirit that I have ever come across occurred when Ron McGregor and I were coming down from a hut in the Dolomites. We were alarmed by the sound of a woman screaming and, rounding a corner, came to an iron ladder. Near the top was a man with a tiny baby in a carrier on his back, at the bottom a very distraught wife. The ladder must have been 40 feet long and as near vertical as makes no difference.

The peak Andy and I did after the Aiguille de la Vanoise I remember only for the extraordinary nature of the rock, which was so friable that between the rock walls we kicked steps up steep slopes of what appeared to be a sort of gritty shale. Towards the top, however, this gave way to red granite and some particularly enjoyable rock climbing, with splendid views over to the Gran Paradiso in Italy.

The next day, we moved on to Cogne and made our way to the camp-site, which turned out to be full. Not far away, however, was a collection of tents – 50 or 60 of them – pitched on what we assumed was an extension of the camp-site but, when we went to the office to pay, they denied any connection and weren't very helpful. On the makeshift camp-site, none of the Italians seemed concerned about the situation and, since it was apparent that some of the tents had been there for a while, we added our tent to the collection.

The next morning, we set off early for the Vittorio Sella Hut so that we could have a good look around and decide what we wanted to do the next day, as the Hut is in a great position with a number of fine peaks nearby. The Hut was crowded, but the company was good, and so we whiled away the hours until it was dark and time to turn in. We had hardly settled down, however, when someone announced that there were lights coming up the hill and, shortly afterwards, the door opened and 30 or 40 more people filed in. We fully expected the two girls, who were running the place, to have a fit at the prospect of fitting this lot into an already crowded hut, but they coped admirably, quickly producing piles of mattresses from somewhere, and soon had the latecomers bedded down, mostly on the floor.

The following day, we did a traverse which took in four peaks, including the Gran Serra. We were pretty fit by this time and moving fast, and, although none of the peaks was difficult, I will always look back on that day as one of the most satisfying days I've had in the Alps. I especially remember some impressive rock on the summit of the Gran Serra, but I was less happy with the state of the snow as we began our descent. It had had the sun on it for much of the day and great expanses of the snowfield looked as if they could avalanche at any minute. Indeed, there was a small avalanche shortly after we began the descent, but fortunately, by this time, we had moved across to a rocky buttress on our right.

I had explained to the wardens at the Vittorio Sella Hut, before we left in the morning, that we were planning a long day and that we might not be back much before eight o'clock in the evening. As it happened, we were back at the Hut by half past seven, but the local mountain rescue team had already been put on the alert.

THE WILD FLOWERS IN THE PYRENEES WERE PARTICULARLY FINE AND WE CONSTANTLY
CAME ACROSS CLUMPS OF THIS LOVELY WHITE LILY.

Fortunately, a quick phone call down to the valley put things right.

We weren't in any particular hurry to get away the next morning, and were half inclined to stay in the Hut for another day and then try the Grivola, but the Dolomites beckoned. It was midday by the time we got down to Cogne where, to our horror, we discovered that our tent –along with all the others on the makeshift site – had vanished. No one from the official camp-site was able to explain what had happened in our absence and the only advice we got was to report the loss to the local police, which is what we did.

The police were very helpful and seemed as concerned as we were at what had happened. We explained that we had lost not only the tent but also our spare clothing, a rope, various maps and guidebooks, and a lot of rock climbing gear, and that, under the terms of our insurance policy, we were required to report the loss to the police and to obtain some kind of acknowledgement. The police said that this could be arranged, but that the loss would have to be formally declared on an official form obtainable only at the stationer's in Cogne. So, up the road we went, only to find that it was the siesta and that the shop wouldn't re-open for another two hours. By this time we were getting pretty fed up, but there was nothing we could do but make the best of it, find a glass of beer and try to be patient, something neither Andy nor I were particularly good at.

Back at the police station, the staff were as helpful as we could have hoped for, but it took ages to itemize all the things we'd lost; each individual piece of protection gear had to be specified, and all this with the Italians speaking very little English and us with no Italian apart, that is, from a few mountaineering terms. It was a weary pair of climbers who left Cogne that night looking for a bivy site, but eventually we found what we wanted and made do. The next day found us in Aosta, where we spent most of the morning replacing the gear we had lost.

As it happens, this frustrating episode preceded a rather amusing one on the way home at the end of the holiday, although we didn't find it quite so funny at the time. When booking our train tickets at Trento, I was careful to make sure that the train we were due to change to, further down the line, was not one on which a supplementary charge would be payable, as replacing so much gear had left us a bit short of ready cash. This was before the days when credit cards were in general use and at a time when getting money at short notice from a bank in England to some remote spot in the Alps could still be difficult – as I had discovered on a previous holiday – and I knew these supplementary charges could be substantial. When I explained at the ticket booking office why we needed to be so careful, the booking clerk was very understanding and he gave me a timetable, underlining the train we were due to change to and writing alongside it something which we understood indicated that the train was not one on which a supplementary charge was payable.

The train in question, when it arrived, was due to go on through Turin. We hadn't been settled in our seats long when the ticket collector came by and, checking our tickets, informed us that the train we were on was a special express and that a supplementary charge was payable. I produced the timetable with its endorsement, but the ticket collector brushed this to one side, stating that the ticket office had been mistaken, at which I pointed out that they were all part of the same railway system and that I was entitled to assume that the right hand knew what the left hand was doing, adding that, in the circumstances, I felt under no obligation to pay a supplementary charge. Quite how the passenger in the seat opposite, who was trying to help us, managed to get all this across to the ticket collector I shall never know as the ticket collector was about as fluent in my language as I was in his. Eventually, however, and muttering that we hadn't heard the last of the business, he left.

Throughout the whole scene, Andy had sat quietly, trying to look as inconspicuous as possible and doubtless wondering what it would be like to spend a night in a Turin jail. Indeed, we got quite a shock when the train pulled into the station at Turin and saw the police waiting on the platform; fortunately for us, they passed us by, and began to question a man who had boarded the train with a wife, 10 children and 23 pieces of luggage.

Once in the Dolomites, Andy and I headed for the Sella Pass. The Pass is in a fantastic position, with several classic Dolomitian climbs close at hand, and I was hoping we might do the traverse of the Cinque Dita and one of the Sella Towers. I have been on the Pass many times over the years, but I am unlikely to forget the last time I was there in a hurry: I had the unenviable task, at the end of a day's climbing, of telephoning my companion's wife to tell her that her husband and son had set out to climb one of the Sella Towers and hadn't returned and, moreover, that the mountain rescue team had been put on alert. Fortunately, from Richmond Upon Thames, she was able to get in touch with her crag-fast family by phone and satisfy herself that there was a good chance that they would survive the night, whereas I, little more than a mile away, had been quite unable to make contact. Apparently, the pair were comfortably settled on a little ledge having got off-route somewhere up the Tower and were, at first, unsure whether they wanted to be rescued at all. By the time all this had been established, the mountain rescue people decided that it was too dark to try to rescue them that night in any case, and they were taken off by helicopter early the next morning.

Our first route from Sella was the traverse of the Cinque Dita, or Five Fingered Peak as climbers often call it, one of whose fingers – the Thumb, if I may put it that way – we left out, as it is quite a bit harder than the rest of the climb and we weren't sure at that stage how we would cope with Dolomitian exposure. At home in the UK, we are inclined to think that a drop of a couple of hundred feet is a long way down whereas, in the Dolomites, it is vital that the climber can cope with a drop beneath his feet of several times that length.

The Cinque Dita was a good route to start with because the climbing was not particularly difficult and we were able to look around and take in the magnificent scenery. The following day, we did two of the Sella Towers and encountered for the first time the vertical walls and long pitches so characteristic of Dolomitian climbing. On the Cinque Dita, we were on the crest of a broken rocky ridge for much of the time and, although the traverse was something like 600 feet long, the exposure didn't bother us; on the Sella Towers, on the other hand, the steepness of the rock wall and the length of the pitches soon brought home the need for steady composure. In the Dolomites, you often find that the descents, usually by abseil, are more serious in some ways than the ascents. You soon get used to the long abseils – and they really are long, often approaching 150 feet – but a lot can go wrong abseiling and they need to be tackled with care.

Our final route before we moved on from Sella was immediately under the cable car route which runs up to Sass Pordoi from the Passo Pordoi. It was a more demanding route technically than anything we'd done so far

THE VIEW OF THE VAJOLET TOWERS FROM ONE OF THE APPROACH PATHS

This area is one of the gems of the Dolomites and is readily accessible from Canazei. It offers almost unlimited rock climbing and plenty of hillwalking of a more serious nature. In the hut, I had the best mushroom omelette I have ever enjoyed!

on this trip, and Andy and I agreed to take alternative leads. What I remember most about the climb is leaving Andy comfortably belayed in a little cave while I did a long rising traverse across a very steep wall, but he led the last pitch, which was certainly the hardest on the climb.

After the Passo Pordoi, we set our sights on the Catinaccio above Canazei which, I think, offers some of the most interesting climbing I've done in the Dolomites – a good variety of moves requiring very concentrated work – and spectacular settings. Our objective was the Vajolet Towers, in particular Torre Stabeler and Torre Piaz. The Stabeler was straightforward apart from a minor rock fall as we abseiled off, but there were a couple of bulges on the vertical wall of Torre Piaz which were considerably harder than the rest of the climb.

From the Catinaccio, we moved on to what proved to be the highlight of the holiday: the ascent of the Marmolada. The highest mountain in the Dolomites, the Marmolada has a substantial glacier on its northern flank and a formidable rock wall to the south. We took the easy route up the glacier, which in those days started immediately above the hut, then right to a rib – which involved some easy rock climbing – and, finally, up a fairly steep snow ridge – with impressive drops on either side – to the summit. Fortunately, the snow was in excellent condition for cramponing and before long we were on the summit plateau where, to our surprise, there was a small hut. Inside, to our utter astonishment, was a small, but well-stocked bar, a notice inviting you to help yourself, and an honesty box complete with a price-list.

The descent of the snow ridge needed care, and both Andy and I remarked on how difficult it would be to check a fall. But we got down safely and, being the first party off the mountain, were greeted by a crowd of visitors who had come up to the hut by chair-lift.

The region in the Dolomites just to the north of the Marmolada is a splendid place for hillwalking, with numerous tracks that take the high ground above Lake Fedaia and open up what must be one of the finest panoramas in Italy. In fact, the Dolomites offer some of the best walking on well-defined, high-level paths in the Alps, with the added advantage that the weather is some of the most reliable. In addition, dotted along the paths, there are huts which can be reached by cable car, and while this means that they are busy at the height of the holiday season, in June – which is a good time to visit the Dolomites – I have sometimes been the only resident. And while the Italians may like to call a hut a 'rifugio', don't let this mislead you: there is nothing primitive about these establishments, and the majority are well-run little hotels, with a choice of accommodation if, occasionally, a somewhat limited one.

When I retired, my colleagues arranged a reception for my wife and I, at which Phyl was presented with a beautiful bouquet of flowers and I a book, Extreme Alpine Rock (Granada, 1979) by Walter Pause and Jürgen Winkler, an excellent review of some of the harder rock climbing in the Alps. I had heard of the book and was delighted to own a copy. In fact, a year later, I was pleased to be able to write to my colleagues and tell them that I had done two of the routes it describes, the Campanile Basso and a more difficult route near Cortina d'Ampezzo, the Punta Fiammes.

The Campanile Basso is one of the great, Dolomitian classics, not because of its intrinsic difficulties – it is not particularly hard by the route we took – but because of the sheer magnificence of the campanile, a natural 'bell

CLIMBERS ON ONE OF THE VAJOLET
TOWERS IN THE DOLOMITES

The climbing is not as hard as it looks as there are
usually plenty of good holds, but the climber must
be able to move steadily up steep rock and not be
too put out by the exposure. You usually descend
by abseiling.

A PARTY ABSEILING OFF THE CAMPANILE
BASSO IN THE DOLOMITES

As the name indicates, the peak is like a bell tower.
The climb is nearly 1,000 feet long. We met the party
on the summit and they agreed that we could share
their abseil ropes, which saved a lot of time on the
descent. The steep wall opposite, with few resting
places, is typical of the Dolomites. It was on the
Campanile Basso that we experienced the short mid-
afternoon hail storm which started without warning
and from a cloudless sky.

THE POPULAR HOLIDAY RESORT OF CORTINA IN THE DOLOMITES

The Punta Fiammes, the climb which gave us so much trouble, is on the huge crag which towers over the town.

tower' close on a 1,000 feet high. When we started the route, it was a perfect day with an Italian blue sky and not a cloud in sight but, as we climbed, one or two clouds began to form around the Campanile Alto nearby. But our luck held for a little while and we were able to enjoy the warm sun on the summit. Then, suddenly it began to hail and the temperature dropped, and in no time at all the summit rocks and all the ledges were covered in hailstones.

I wasn't too worried because I'd experienced summer hailstorms in the Dolomites before and they had never lasted long. Not surprisingly, however, my companion was more concerned as he was new to the Dolomites, and the prospect of abseiling down 1,000 feet of rock, with hailstones piled high on all the ledges, seemed rather daunting. Fortunately, the storm only lasted a few minutes before the sun came out again, and in half an hour there wasn't a hailstone to be seen.

The abseil off the Campanile Basso is quite straightforward, but I've done one or two hairy abseils in my time, including one where you finish up on the end of 150 feet of rope and about 15 feet off the cliff face. When you've collected your wits and stopped spinning, you have to start swinging in towards the rock face until you can grab one of the pitons hammered into the wall and pull yourself on to a ledge. We were lucky on the Basso. Following us up the climb was a large party of Austrian mountain guides enjoying a holiday, and they kindly let us use their abseil ropes. We met them again in the hut that evening, and what a cheerful group they were!

The ascent of the Punta Fiammes, on the other hand, was a completely different experience, and we found ourselves in some strange situations before our adventures were over. We climbed it almost by chance. I'd always wanted to do the Spigolo Giallo, or 'Yellow Edge', an outstanding route on a Dolomitian tower high in the mountains above Cortina, but when we got there it was quite out of condition. While we were ambling around, wondering what to do, we bumped into another couple of Brits, one of whom – Mark – I knew from my Tremadoc days and who, like us, had been hoping to climb the Spigolo Giallo; and since we all felt that it wasn't worth hanging about waiting for the weather to improve, we looked for an interesting climb lower down and settled on the Punta Fiammes.

We split into two ropes of two, and Mark, who was to lead me up the climb, decided to take an alternative, rather more difficult, start which converged with the standard start after a few pitches. It is a long route – something approaching 1,000 feet, I seem to recall – and things began to go wrong from the beginning. Mark had run out all the rope on the first pitch – a long rising traverse – before he could find a belay, and I had just started to follow him when the small block of rock I was moving around broke away and went crashing down on to the scree below. Fortunately, I was able to hang on to firmer rock with my left hand while I swung out of the way of the falling block, which was about the size of a small suitcase.

Our two parties met again where the two starts converge and, for a while, we made steady, if slow, progress. Gradually, however, our companions on the other rope began to find the difficulties of the climb and the considerable exposure too much and, at the crux of the climb, they decided they couldn't continue without support. We were now in some difficulty because time was getting on and we still had several hundred feet

A PARTY SETTING OFF FROM THE REFUGIO AURONZO, A POPULAR HUT ABOVE MISURINA

of rock to climb. None of us felt like trying to descend so, with a rope of four, we carried on with the ascent, which Mark led superbly.

By the time we reached the summit, it was almost dark and, having been on the go for about 12 hours, we considered bivouacking where we were. But it was getting chilly and, in the end, we decided to try to get down to valley, which we managed, eventually coming across a disused railway we hoped would lead us down to Cortina. With our head torches now barely a glimmer, we set off down the track only to find ourselves in a tunnel. Fortunately, it wasn't a very long one, but we were soon confronted with a second tunnel which seemed to go on forever. Here, we were literally feeling the way with our feet as we could sense that the surface was dangerously uneven. By the time we emerged into the open, we had had more than enough and we stopped at a concrete blockhouse at the side of the track – a relic, I imagine, of the First World War – where we dossed down for what remained of the night. Being the old man of the party, I was given the ropes to lie on; it was bitterly cold and we shivered in unison until dawn.

Cortina d'Ampezzo, as well as being a major climbing centre and ski resort, has a great deal to offer the hillwalker. From the beautifully situated lake at Misurina, no more than a short bus ride from Cortina, there is a scenic road which leads up to the Rifugio Auronzo. The scenery from here, past the Rifugio Lavaredo to the Rifugio Locatelli – taking in, as it does, the Tre Cime di Lavaredo – is generally held to be amongst the finest in the Dolomites. Cortina is also a very handsome town, with a baroque church of which – if the frequency with which this landmark appears on postcards and in books about the area is any indication – the townsfolk are very proud.

The first time I went to Cortina, I was intrigued to find that the picture on the postcard I bought to send home – a picture of the celebrated church – was a reproduction of a painting by Edward Harrison Compton (1881–1960), son of Edward Theodore Compton, the painter so highly esteemed in the Alps, and I was pleased to see that the painter's skill was warmly acknowledged on the postcard. A year or two later, the bookshops in the town were prominently displaying the same picture, this time on the dust-jacket of a large coffee-table book about Cortina and the surrounding country.

The main town in the Brenta Dolomites, where we climbed the Campanile Basso, is Madonna di Campiglio. While the town might lack some of Cortina's character, it is a first rate centre for both climbing and walking, and has the added attraction of being nestled been two different types of country: to the east, it is typically Dolomitian limestone country whereas, to the west, the rock is what I believe the geologists call adamellite, a striking black-and-white rock made up, principally, of quartz and feldspar.

Adamellite is named after Adamello, a mountain to the west of Madonna di Campiglio, which seems to consist almost entirely of this particular rock. Ron McGregor and I tried to climb Adamello on one of our trips, but there was a violent electric storm during the night we spent in the hut, and when we woke up in the morning, much to our disappointment, there was a lot of new snow on the higher slopes which put climbing out of the question. We were luckier, however, when we did the trek round the Adamello , a very worthwhile mountain excursion which took us, I seem to recall, three days, before we finished at Passo Tonale.

Another short mountain tour, one that I did on my own, was the trek round Monte Viso, a fine, well-shaped mountain which lies just south of the border between France and Italy, but much of whose appeal depends on its position south of the main Alpine chain. The magnificent, wide-ranging view it provides stretches, on a good day, all the way from the Savoy to the Dolomites.

Monte Viso may seem a bit out of the way to walkers used to the main Alpine centres, but you can easily reach it by car from Briançon and the countryside you pass through en route is very picturesque, especially around Château Queyras. I have rarely enjoyed a mountain excursion as much: the weather was good, there were lovely views at every turn in the path, and the mountain flowers were the best I have seen outside the Pyrenees. On the way round, I met only one other walker, a young Englishman who had started at Toulon and was working his way to Chamonix.

The hut was relatively quiet when I arrived, with only two parties who were planning to climb the Viso the following day. When I set out from Briançon at the beginning of the trip, I had no intention of climbing anything. My serious mountaineering days were over and I had resolved that, henceforth, I would be content with easy walking. But, as the evening went on, I became more and more envious of the climbers until, eventually plucking up the courage, I asked the warden if there was any chance of hiring a pair of crampons. Luckily he was able to fix me up.

The Italian parties started at first light with me not far behind, but there was a lot of loose rock about and it soon became advisable to keep to one side. From then on, I made my own way up the mountain, enjoying the steadily widening view of the Alps to the north. The climbing was never difficult and, apart from one short stretch, nothing more than what I would call serious scrambling. There was one small snowfield shortly after we left the hut, but this hardly justified putting on the crampons.

The journey back to Ailefroide, where I was due to rejoin some friends, was more exciting than I had bargained for. By this time, I had given up driving on the Continent and, when I was on my own, relied on public transport and the occasional hitchhike. On the whole, I have enjoyed hitchhiking. It is often nice to have company for a while, though now and then I have felt that I would, perhaps, have been safer on the mountain.

The very first lift I got on the way to Ailefroide convinced me of this. No sooner had I got into the car than the driver asked me if I liked being driven fast, and when I gave a very firm 'No', his reply left me in little doubt as to what I was in for. 'My motto,' he said, 'is "always first", and my hobby is fast driving,' before going on to add that if, as a mountaineer, I was prepared to take risks on the hills, why shouldn't he do the same on the roads. By this time, he was so busy demonstrating his risk-taking capabilities that I thought it best not to upset him by pointing out that the comparison is hardly a valid one. After about 20 minutes – which aged me more than 20 years of climbing – he stopped at a café where he was due to deliver a coffee machine. No sooner had he turned his back than I grabbed my rucksack and ran.

Another hairy hitchhiking episode happened when I was walking down from Pont, a little village south of Aosta, and a popular centre for climbing the Gran Paradiso. The road was quiet, and a young couple stopped and offered me a lift. The vehicle struck me as being very old and somewhat dilapidated, but I could hardly refuse their kind offer. Once we were on our way, however, it soon became apparent from their conversation that, not only was the car old and dilapidated, it was unreliable as well and given to breaking down at frequent intervals. It was equally clear that the girl had had quite enough of the wretched machine and, after mentioning that they were on their honeymoon, she began to catalogue some of the things that had gone wrong so far. She was in full flow when her husband announced, almost nonchalantly, that the brakes had failed.

It must have been our lucky day because, after screeching downhill for another 200 yards and trying to slow the car down using the hand brake, we came to a track leading into a forest and cruised up that, eventually coming to a halt. The couple then started a blazing row and I took the opportunity to slip out of the car and get on my way. What happened to them subsequently I can't say: I plodded down that road for another two hours, but the car never passed me.

MY HOME-MADE TENTLET – WEIGHING JUST ONE POUND SEVEN OUNCES – ON THE TREK
ROUND MONTE VISO, THE MOUNTAIN IN THE BACKGROUND

This was one of my first solo mountain holidays after retirement and my intention was to take my time
ambling round the mountain before heading for the Dolomites. But the Viso was so attractive that I ended up
climbing it.

CHAPTER NINE

Big tents and little tents

Being small and lightly built I have never been able to carry the huge loads that some of my stronger friends seem to manage, and the introduction of the Gortex bivouac sack, with its waterproof but breathable properties, seemed to provide an alternative to the conventional mountain tent, saving perhaps two or three pounds in weight. It was worth a try at least and, having bought one, I was soon able to put it to the test above Misurina in the Dolomites.

It was a perfect night and we were late getting into our sleeping bags, preferring to sit for a while and enjoy the spectacle of the lights in the valley below. Shortly after midnight, however, the wind got up and it was soon blowing a full gale. Then it began to rain, a heavy, driving rain with a wind so strong that I was afraid it would tear the bivy sack to pieces. Throughout the night, I struggled to stop the sack from flapping and I expected to feel the damp creep through the fabric at any minute, finding it difficult to imagine that any material could stand up to such punishment for long. It was an anxious night, but I wriggled out of the bivy sack the next morning almost as dry as when I got in. There was just one bit around the top of my sleeping bag where some rain had found its way through, but this was simply because I hadn't completely closed the zip. I still have the sack and, when I stopped using it on the hills, I put it to good use on my boat where, for several years, it kept my sleeping bag free of that clammy feeling which a sleeping bag so quickly acquires at sea. So, one way or another, that bivy sack has served me very well indeed.

I've never felt it's wise to have a bivy sack completely closed when you're inside, but if you don't zip it up completely you are left with the problem of managing the gap as, however carefully you try to arrange it, some rain will invariably find its way inside, usually somewhere around your neck. On one trip to the Alps, when we climbed Pic Coolidge and some other peaks in the Écrins, I tried the trick of hanging my cagoule from my ice-axe so that it provided some protection for my head and shoulders. It was far from a perfect arrangement, but it was promising enough to make me think that it might be worth making a head-and-shoulder canopy for use in conjunction with a bivy sack.

After experimenting with one or two makeshift arrangements, I bought a suitable length of tent fabric, the lightest available, and my wife and I set to work. The first thing was to decide how we should cut the cloth for the canopy and fortunately, while we were working this out, we realised that, for another three or four ounces in weight, we could make a complete 'tentlet'. By the end of the afternoon, this is precisely what we had: a fine, little bivy tent, which I was to use for the next 25 years – the first time at La Bérarde in the French Alps, and the last on the Lairig Ghru in Scotland. With pegs and poles, it weighed one pound seven ounces, and the ladies dress zip which we used to close the flaps has functioned perfectly for over a quarter of a century.

Used together with a bivy sack and a small carry mat, the bivy tent provided an astonishing amount of protection and could be pitched in places where there simply wasn't room to put up the smallest conventional mountain tent. Several times over the years, mainly due to its low profile, it weathered storms which severely damaged expensive tents nearby and, on one occasion near Saint-Gervais, I emerged, dry as a bone, to find half the campers huddled in the washrooms, having abandoned their tents during the night.

The tentlet caused a lot of amusement on those rare occasions when I used it on public camp-sites. The first time was in the French Alps, where the camp-site I had chosen had two different tariffs, one for 'grandes tentes' (big family tents) and the other for 'petites tentes' (little mountain tents). When asked about size, I said that mine was a small tent, adding that it was probably the smallest tent in France, whereupon the site manager asked if he could see it. When he opened it out, he started to laugh, exclaiming that he had seen bigger pocket handkerchieves and that he couldn't possibly charge me for a thing like that, – all this in French, of course.

On another occasion in the French Alps, this time at a camp-site near Megève, I returned at the end of the day to find a number of children walking around the tent, apparently discussing what it was for. I moved in close enough to hear what they were saying without disturbing them, and was just in time to hear them decide that it must be 'pour le chien'. And so, my splendid little bivy tent was, after all, nothing more than a portable dog kennel.

CHAPTER TEN
High jinx on the Cevedale

The Cevedale is a mountain I'd never heard of until the day before I climbed it on a holiday I never intended to take. For five weeks that summer, I'd been helping Bob Percival sail his yacht, *Andata*, around Greece, and at the end of the trip I had planned to return home by train, possibly stopping off along the way if somewhere took my fancy.

One of the ideas I'd been toying with was to spend a few days walking in the Julian Alps, an area I was not familiar with but which I'd heard was very attractive. The summer in Greece had, however, been one of the hottest on record, and I began to wonder whether I might find the weather in the Julian Alps too hot for comfort. The more I thought about it, the more sensible it seemed to head for one of the snowy areas of the High Alps, and I finally decided to try the Ortles Group in Italy, or somewhere in the vicinity.

It was a region I hadn't visited before, but it seemed, from what I'd read, to offer the possibility of some interesting walking and perhaps a climb on one or two of the easier mountains. The night journey by train from Athens to Milan was slow and tedious, and it was a relief to spend a couple of hours wandering around Milan, stretching my legs. From Milan, I took the bus to Ponte di Legno, a lovely little town at the foot of the Passo di Gavia. I'd been over the Pass by car on an earlier trip, and remember thinking it might be a pleasant pass to walk over one day as it was high, not too busy, and there is a convenient rifugio at the top.

It was, indeed, a delightful walk, with splendid mountain scenery on either side, and, still more striking, one of the finest displays of roadside flowers I've ever seen. I've been over the Pass once since, in the opposite direction, and the view as you drop down towards Ponte di Legno is particularly impressive. Unfortunately, on that occasion, I was so preoccupied avoiding cyclists, who came hurtling down the Pass, that I had little time for the scenery.

In those days, getting about by bus from Ponte di Legno could be a tricky business if you didn't know the ropes. For some buses you bought the ticket on the bus, whereas for other journeys you got them at the bus station in the centre of the town. On one occasion, when I was planning to catch the 7 a.m. bus to Milan the next morning, I found that the ticket office closed in the early evening and didn't open again until eight o'clock in the morning. When I expressed some surprise at this rather odd arrangement, I was told that there was really no problem, as the little inn a couple of hundred yards away sold tickets until closing time – a perfect arrangement, if you happened to know about it!

The rifugio at the top of the Passo di Gavia was crowded when I arrived, but I slept well enough and, the next morning, made my way down to Santa Caterina Valfurva, where I had a lazy day and, in true sybaritic tradition, found a hotel for the night.

The following day, I set off up the valley towards the nearest hut, intending to do nothing more than look in and return to Santa Caterina in the late afternoon. I'd been walking for about an hour when two vehicles passed me, one of which stopped 100 yards or so ahead, then began to back towards me, the driver beckoning me to join them. I was delighted because I had hardly spoken to anyone apart from ticket collectors and bus drivers since I left Bob at Athens.

The group – they were Italians – was soon quizzing me about how old I was, where I had come from, and why I was in the Ortles. When they learned that I'd climbed in various parts of Italy, they said that there were three climbers in the other car who were planning to climb the Cevedale the following day, and that I must meet them. The rest of the party, it seems, had no intention of going any further than the hut. They were a very friendly bunch, and in due course I was introduced to the three climbers, who were working out how they would cope with the problems they were likely to meet on the Cevedale the next day.

Gradually, I found I was being drawn more and more into the discussion, until eventually they suggested that I should join them, an invitation which I declined as gracefully as I could, explaining that I hadn't climbed for some time and was getting on a bit. Furthermore, I had no ice-axe and no crampons. However, I was enjoying their company, and it seemed both sensible and courteous to stay at the hut and spend the evening with them. This was soon arranged and, after a good meal during which the wine flowed freely, the prospect of joining them on the Cevedale became more and more attractive. Crampons, it seems, weren't really necessary and when one of the group disappeared then returned with an ice-axe he'd borrowed from the guardian of the rifugio, I somehow forgot my earlier resolve and agreed to climb with them.

We were away from the hut early the next morning, and it was only then that I saw what the climb involved. By the route my companions had chosen to take, it was entirely a snow and ice climb: a stretch across a glacier, followed by a fairly long snow slope at a reasonable angle leading more or less directly to the summit; in all, perhaps, about 2,500 feet of climbing.

The Cevedale is over 12,000 feet high and, at first sight, the climb appeared to be straightforward enough, but soon after we left the hut it became apparent that it wasn't quite as trouble-free as it looked when the leader, moving across snow which seemed as firm as you could hope for, went into a crevasse up to his waist. We soon had him out, but after that we paid a lot more attention to the state of the snow, a thin covering hiding countless ice chasms just below the surface – all of which helped to confirm my belief that there is no such thing as an uncrevassed glacier.

Once across the glacier, we enjoyed some good climbing up firm snow, but we were held up now and then when the third climber on the rope began to have trouble with his crampons, which kept coming loose. Adjusting crampons on a snow slope is never particularly easy, and I gathered later that this was the first time the climber had worn a pair. When we began to climb the snow slope, we were the leading party, but we were overtaken by a number of other parties while the crampons were being adjusted, something which introduces the risk of being carried down the mountain should one of the parties above fall. I have never seen this happen, but I once saw a climber badly injured on a climb in the Stubai Alps in Austria when someone above dropped his ice-axe.

It was quite early in the day when we reached the summit, and we spent an hour or so soaking up the view and generally enjoying ourselves in that convivial way Italians have of making you feel as though you have known them all your life. Then, to my surprise – and, I think, to the surprise of the other two climbers – the leader announced that he was going to carry on to the other summit. This was a puzzling decision because the other summit was about 20 feet lower than the one we were on, and lay at some distance along a knife-edge ridge of pristine snow, with drops of about 2,000 feet on either side. Moreover, no other party on the summit of the Cevedale that morning had shown the slightest interest in traversing across to the other summit.

However, the rather mild remonstrations of the other Italians appeared to have no effect on the leader's resolve and, as a guest, it was difficult for me to do more than point out that what he was proposing was very much harder than any climbing we'd done on the way up. Intent on trying the ridge regardless, it wasn't long before he had run out about 20 feet of rope. At this point, I thought that I should make sure that the other Italians knew what to do if he fell off – essentially to arrest the fall quickly by jumping down opposite sides of the ridge – but I got the impression that they preferred not to think about this possibility. Fortunately, after running out a few more feet of rope, the leader realized that the traverse was harder than he had bargained for and he came back, but not before some anxious moments as he turned around.

The descent went without a hitch, but the snow was beginning to soften and particular care was needed as we crossed the glacier. Once off the glacier, the Italians embraced me warmly, and we all agreed that we had had an exciting day – apparently a little too exciting for one of them who remarked, sounding a little more earnest, I think, than he intended, that it was the first time he'd been on a mountain and that he would make sure that it was the last.

ANNECY, A DELIGHTFUL PLACE IN WHICH TO UNWIND AFTER AN
ENERGETIC HOLIDAY IN THE ALPS

CHAPTER ELEVEN

Autumn days in the Alps

Ron McGregor and I were, you might say, getting on a bit – we were well into our sixties and seventies – but that seemed no reason for giving up climbing in the Alps. A bit old, perhaps, for the North Wall of the Eiger and such like, but just the right age for some of the lesser peaks. That's the way we saw it, anyway, and we didn't take a lot of convincing.

The two trips we did – the first one when we climbed the Gran Paradiso and a later one when we concentrated on passes – turned out to be among the most enjoyable we've had together. This was mainly, I suppose, because we were happy to take our time and didn't try to cram too much in, but more particularly, I think, because we were prepared to accept that our Alpine days were numbered and therefore to be savoured all the more.

Our visit to the Gran Paradiso started off rather unusually. On arriving at the Rifugio Vittorio Emanuele, we were told that it was completely full and that we would have to make do with a bed in the annex. This sounded a bit ominous at first but, once there, we found that the only other occupants were two Italian climbers who turned out to be very interesting company. Moreover, the annex was actually quite snug and I couldn't help comparing this with the conditions in the main hut the first time I climbed the Paradiso when, at bed time, I was allocated a mattress in one of the corridors. Not that this was anything to fuss about in itself as I'd slept in hut corridors once or twice before – but never immediately in front of the only toilet facilities in the hut where, throughout a very long night, climber after climber stepped over or shuffled past me.

Looking back on that first ascent of the Gran Paradiso, with a fellow member of the North London Mountaineering Club, I realize that it was an odd trip in more ways than one. Then a comparative newcomer to Alpine climbing, I'd taken the advice of more experienced colleagues and invested in some thermal underwear, and the Paradiso – one of the highest mountains in Italy – seemed the ideal opportunity to try it out.

I'd never worn long johns, thermal or otherwise, before. We were among the first parties to leave the hut and we made good time for a while, but I soon began to realize that, even on the glacier, the morning was far warmer than I'd expected – it wasn't long before I began to sweat and itch – and that something would have to be done about it. But there isn't much you can do about troublesome underwear once you've got it on but take it off again, and this is what I was eventually forced to do, starting with my crampons and steadily stripping off until I found myself, at six o'clock in the morning, in the middle of a glacier somewhere in North Italy, stark naked. I am happy to leave the details of the performance to your imagination but it was very obvious that the Italian climbers who passed by while it was going on enjoyed it immensely.

Back in the annex with Ron, the evening passed all too quickly; we had the company of two friendly Italians, one of whom spoke excellent English, and comfortable quarters for the night. After we'd settled in and eaten, Ron and I started browsing through our guidebooks, trying to decide where we should head for once we'd done the Paradiso. I was leafing through a guidebook on the Eastern Alps, when the Italian who spoke English came across and mentioned that he was in the middle of revising the Italian guidebook to that particular region, and that he had all the available guidebooks for reference during the process, including the one I was studying. He warned us to be careful when using the book in question, and to check the details locally before starting a climb, as some of the route descriptions were misleading. Then, just to give us a bit of extra encouragement, he looked up one of the longest and most serious routes and highlighted a critical point where the climber must move left, and not right as stated.

Shortly after we left the hut the following day, I noticed how much the snow and ice conditions on the Gran Paradiso had changed since I first climbed it. Where there used to be gentle slopes of firm snow, ideal for cramponing, there was now a mixture of snow and ice, with a crevasse showing here and there; and, rather than the fairly even slopes of earlier years, height now tended to be gained through a mixture of more or less level stretches of glacier interspersed with steeper sections. Still, it was fairly undemanding climbing and the weather was settled so we were able enjoy it even though we were aware that it was a long route and that we hadn't got the reserves we once had.

On the summit, the view was as fine as ever: the peaks nearby are all quite striking and the distant views, especially to the north, are superb. On the way down, we decided we'd had enough of snow and ice and for the last 1,500 feet or so we left the glacier and took to the nearby rock, enjoying some pleasant scrambling en route.

A few days later we climbed the Ciamarella which, I remember, included a stretch of easy glacier, a shaly traverse, and some good solid rock to finish. But what the Ciamarella lacked in quality of climbing was more than made up for that day by the magnificence of the scene, both in its clarity and its breadth. Without a doubt it was the finest Alpine vista I have ever seen, and I subsequently heard from a friend, who had been on a mountain not very far away on the same day, that he had found the scene equally memorable.

Our next aim was to see something of the country to the south of Monte Rosa and the Mezzalama Hut seemed to be a promising place to head for. The approach to the Hut itself was enough to make the trip worthwhile: along the lovely Val d'Ayas followed by the long pull up a lateral moraine, where the scenery was some of the most savage Ron and I had seen in the Alps.

The Hut was what we expected it to be: small and with an air of seriousness about it. Shortly after we arrived, another group of climbers turned up, obviously very tired and clearly thankful to be down. They had come across from Zermatt and had found much of the route harder than they had bargained for, with long stretches of raw ice where they had expected good cramponing snow, a pattern becoming all too common in the Alps.

The descent from the Hut the next morning was as interesting as the ascent, with the view gradually widening to take in more and more of the hills to the south. This was the end of our holiday and the last of the serious climbing Ron and I did together – if, that is, you measure seriousness by the ascent of mountain peaks. Of the peaks, passes and glaciers, we had done plenty of peaks and glaciers over the years and it was now time to concentrate on the passes, which is essentially what Ron and I did on our final Alpine holiday together.

Realising that we had some serious backpacking ahead of us, we started training, with long walks on the South Downs above South Harting which soon settled into regular walks from Harting to Cocking and back, carrying increasingly heavy loads. Then, for a change, we carried the same loads across the slump areas from Axmouth to Lyme Regis, which was a disappointing trip because for much of the time the country was so heavily wooded that we saw little of the sea.

Our final training excursion was to Scotland and is particularly memorable because we crossed the Lairig Ghru, a mountain walk I'd wanted to do ever since I first heard about it as a teenager. Having crossed the Lairig Ghru, we had been planning to take in Loch Avon and have a look at the Shelter Stone, but the weather steadily deteriorated and so we cut our losses and made our way down to the Lake District, where we climbed Great Gable. It was during this trip that I noticed that the fabric of my little bivy tent was getting a bit stiff and I couldn't be sure how strong it was. It had been a sturdy little companion and had kept me safe in many a mountain storm.

Our last alpine holiday together started at Annecy, as attractive a starting point as you could hope for, and from there we made our way to Le Grand-Bornand, where we camped for the night. The following day, we pushed up into the hills, eventually bedding down on a pass which I seem to remember was the Col des Annes. Our intention so far had been to follow the hill paths to Cluses and then go on to Chamonix, but the weather out towards Chamonix looked unsettled so we decided to cut our losses and try the Alps to the south of Grenoble, where Valjouffrey was supposed to be very attractive.

WHERE NEXT? THE FRENCH ALPS NOT FAR FROM VALLOUISE

I am astonished to see how small my rucksack looks in this photograph, as it contained everything I needed for a fortnight's mountaineering, including a tent, my sleeping bag and wet weather gear. Although we had no plans to climb peaks, we did cross a number of high passes and often camped at over 6,000 feet.

ONE OF OUR CAMP-SITES ON THE LAST CLIMBING TRIP RON MCGREGOR AND I MADE TO THE ALPS

A splendid finish to our Alpine days, as we were both in our seventies by this time. We had walked from Vallouise intending to make our way to Gap, the nearest town of any size. After Le Pas de la Cavale, we had to descend something like 2,000 feet before we could find level ground on which to pitch our tents. We eventually found what we wanted, more or less, but the camp-site was not quite as idyllic as the picture suggests as we failed to spot the dead sheep lying behind a rock not far away. There was a spectacular storm on the hills on the other side of the valley that evening.

Valjouffrey, though a steep-sided valley and rather closed in, was well worth the visit and I especially remember the view of the Pic d' Olan and the climb up to the Fond Turbat Hut. No sooner had we stepped into the Hut than the warden greeted us with the question, 'Messieurs, quelle est solipsisme?', which took us back a bit because we weren't actually sure what solipsism was and were even less sure why she was so desperate to know. Eventually, after quite a struggle with the language, we discovered that she had been listening to a radio programme on philosophy and that the word had cropped up. We were the only people in the Hut as the party who had been due to stay there over the weekend had cancelled, so it is perhaps not surprising that she had turned to philosophy for company.

The next area we visited was the Oisans, taking the bus from Bourg d'Oisons up the 20 or so zigzags to the celebrated ski resort of L'Alpe d'Huez. It may offer excellent skiing, but the resort hardly enhances the scenery. Fortunately, soon after we left the village, La Meije came into view, another outstanding Alpine panorama. I seem to recall that La Meije was the last of the big alpine peaks to be climbed and it was not hard to see why. We camped that night close to Le Chazelet and ambled down to La Grave the following day with the mountain before us most of the way.

From La Grave we hitchhiked to Ailefroide, and from there took our time walking up to Pré de Madame Carle, enjoying the fine view of the Barre des Écrins on the way. The next day, we made our way to Vallouise and as, by this time, we were getting reasonably fit – fit, that is, for two old gents – we decided to try something a little more ambitious. Not that we had done too badly so far, given that most nights we had camped at around the 7,000 foot mark and on some days hadn't seen another walker or climber. Our plan now was to climb Le Pas de la Cavale, camp there for the night and then head for Gap, the nearest town of any consequence.

From Vallouise we got a lift to Entre-les-Aigues, where the serious part of the excursion began. It was easy enough at first, but became increasingly strenuous as we approached Le Pas de la Cavale. The last thousand feet or so up to the top of the Pass were more serious than we'd expected and saw us tackling a path which zigzagged up a steep slope of loose shale. With no loads on our backs this wouldn't have worried us too much, but moving up such a steep slope while negotiating the turns in the path and carrying substantial loads was decidedly tricky. This last stretch took us over three hours, which gives some indication of how careful we had to be: a slip would almost certainly have proved fatal.

The top of the Pass turned out to be far from the ideal camp-site we'd hoped for, being narrow and very rocky, but we enjoyed the traverse along the ridge before beginning the descent, all the time looking for a level spot to pitch our tents. We must have descended nearly 2,000 feet before we found what we needed. There was a sickeningly strong smell of sheep about the place but it had to do. We had travelled far enough for one day. It was a wonderful camp-site and despite the smell we relaxed in the evening sunlight, soaking up the view and feeling rather pleased with the way things were going. We discovered the cause of the smell the following morning when we left the camp-site: not far away lay the carcass of a sheep, and in an advanced state of decay.

Just before we turned in, however, ominous clouds began to gather over the mountains to the north and it wasn't long before they were engulfed in a violent storm, accompanied by a fine display of thunder and lightning. As alpine storms go it was probably nothing extraordinary, but I remember feeling glad I wasn't there. These storms are often very local, sometimes raging over a single peak, but they can be just as devastating as less localised bad weather.

The journey to Gap the following day was a pleasant change from the energetic days we'd had on the trip so far and, after looking around the town, we took the train to Chamonix where we had planned to end our holiday. Returning to Chamonix was as much a sentimental journey as anything and we were happy to spend our last day in the Alps on the Aiguilles Rouges, ambling between the Brévent and La Flégère, recalling old adventures.

It was nearly 50 years since my first visit to Chamonix, and Ron had probably known it almost as long. Our connection with the old town must have shown, somehow or other, as we were stopped in the street by a photographer who said she was a journalist writing about the Chamonix of bygone years and asked to take our photograph. I have often wondered how she used it and what she wrote about us.

SPRING IN THE PYRENEES

RON WEIGHING UP WHAT LIES AHEAD

It was pretty wild country, fairly typical of the Pyrenees, and we were carrying quite
heavy loads for two old age pensioners.

CHAPTER TWELVE
The Pyrenees and the Picos de Europa

My first visit to the Pyrenees was with a friend who was a keen botanist and we stayed at Panticosa. We were fortunate with our choice of venue, which is set in some fine mountain scenery and, with a very cold winter having produced plenty of snow, the hills looked particularly inviting. The skiers at Formigal and the other ski resorts were having the time of their lives. I was tempted to join them, but knew from past experience with my family in Austria that I would only twist my knee. While the heavy snowfall restricted my walking a bit, it made the landscape look very picturesque and some of the photographs I took there are amongst my best.

It was many years before I visited the area again, with Ron McGregor; it was his first trip to these mountains. We were lucky and managed to do one of the finest treks in the Pyrenees, up the Anisclo Canyon and down the Ordesa Canyon, taking three days over the trip and carrying all our food and bivy gear with us. It was a fantastic excursion made all the more interesting by the profusion of wild flowers, but it was a serious undertaking nevertheless, with a lot of energetic walking and some quite exposed scrambling as we dropped down into the Ordesa Canyon. Until the very end of the journey, when we were well down the Canyon and bumped into a Swedish couple, we didn't see a single person.

As it happened, our encounter with the Swedes was a very fortunate one because they were keen bird watchers, armed with both field-glasses and a high-powered telescope, and the following day they took us to the head of a pass where we saw a pair of lammergeyers in flight. The lammergeyer is the largest bird native to Europe with a wingspan of up to nine feet. We were told that they are capable of carrying the thigh bone of an ox high into the air, which they then drop onto a rock hoping to shatter it so that they can get at the bone

THE PIC DU MIDI D'OSSAU PHOTOGRAPHED FROM THE COL DU POURTALET
The popular Pyrenean ski resort of Formigal is not far away.

marrow. Whether this is true or not, I can't say, but I must check my mountaineering insurance policy to see if I'm covered should I have the misfortune to be hit on the head by a bone dropped by a careless lammergeyer.

The highlight of that holiday was undoubtedly climbing the Pic du Midi d'Ossau, one of the most attractive mountains in the Pyrenees. Not only is it a very striking peak, it is also magnificently situated – close to the top of the Col du Pourtalet – and the ascent is one that any climber must simply itch to do. The climb, which we decided to solo, was interesting; for most of the way, the rock climbing wasn't particularly difficult, but it finished with a snowfield which, having no ice-axe myself, I decided to leave to Ron.

Almost everyone I know who has climbed or walked in the Pyrenees has found himself drawn back to them, often again and again, and it is natural to compare them with the Alps. With one or two exceptions, such as the Pic du Midi d'Ossau, the Pyrenean peaks have never seemed to me to be so immediately striking as many peaks in the Alps. The appeal of the Pyrenees seems to me to lie as much in the valleys as in the mountains above, as the Pyrenean valleys are beautiful in a way that few Alpine valleys can match. This is due to a number of things: the abundance of deciduous trees, which cloak the valley sides; the wide range of shrubs, often with light-reflecting leaves; the occasional pencil cedar, which gives a new dimension to the landscape; and, most of all, the quality of the light.

On my very first visit to the Pyrenees, we walked in the hills just beyond Luchon where, on the opposite side of the valley, the hillside was covered in deciduous trees and I was left wondering what the scene would look like in the Autumn when the leaves had turned colour and there was a dusting of snow on the mountaintops. I had seen this effect in the Lake District and in Scotland on various occasions, and it isn't something you quickly forget. Recently, Ivan Barnett – with whom I've often climbed and sailed – and I went to the Pyrenees to see how things looked in the autumn and how fortunate we were: it was late in October, the weather was perfect – apart from a light shower as we crossed the Col du Somport – and for much of the trip we enjoyed brilliant autumn colours in the valleys and sun-lit snow on the higher peaks.

Over the years, I had heard a lot about the attractions of the Picos de Europa – the group of mountains in Spain roughly south-west of Santander – and I felt it was time I paid them a visit. Now well into my eighties, I had accepted that my climbing days were over, but I was still good for a bit of walking; so, starting at Barcelona, I worked my way across the Pyrenees, mostly by bus, until I came to Pau. From Pau, I travelled south over the Col du Somport to Jaca and, feeling like a bit of coastal walking, I carried on to Santander. The coastal walking was rather disappointing, but at Santander I was within easy reach of the Picos so, the following day, I took the bus to Potes, a very attractive little town in a magnificent setting, more or less surrounded by craggy limestone hills.

The next day, I set off walking towards Fuente De, not very sure what to do as there were so many attractive options. I had hardly left Potes behind when a car stopped and I was offered a lift. When I asked the driver where he would advise me to spend the day, he mentioned that the cable car at Fuente De was running, which made up my mind, especially as he said he had no particular plans and was happy to take me there.

Once in Fuente De, the cable car soon whisked me up to the top of a spectacular limestone cirque and for the next hour I was quite happy just to wander about and admire the view. But then, spotting a track which led towards the valley, I decided to explore. The walk down to the road, which took me most of the morning, was delightful – the wild flowers were at their best, especially the gentians, which in places literally carpeted the hillside – and I didn't see another soul until, in the last mile or so, I came across a group of workmen repairing the track.

There were still three things I wanted to do before I left Spain: see something of the interior; visit El Escorial, the royal palace near Madrid; and see the Alhambra at Granada. The journey by bus across Spain was interesting, but the hilly country was not as striking as I'd imagined it to be because the hills tend to rise gently out of the already high plateau. El Escorial was impressive because of its sheer bulk, but the light was poor when I went around the Alhambra and I was rather disappointed.

However, there was a pleasant surprise awaiting me on the following day, the last day of my holiday. I had taken the bus up to the Sierra Nevada ski resort and, unsure what to do next, had started to walk up a little road which wound its way up the hillside. As the road unwound before me, more and more of the sierras were revealed until, eventually, Mulhacén, the highest mountain in Spain, came into view. The hills of the Sierra Nevada do not have the appeal of the Pyrenees, being rather dark and shaly, but the breadth of the view was impressive.

On and on I went, until the road finally petered out at the upper station of a ski-lift. From there, some easy scrambling took me to the top of Pico Veleta which, at something over 11,000 feet, is one of the highest mountains in Spain. Words can never quite express my feelings as I rested for a while, soaking up the view, but it was, for me, a memorable occasion and a very satisfying way to end 70 years of mountaineering.

THE SPLENDIDLY SITUATED HUT FROM WHICH RON MCGREGOR
AND I CLIMBED THE PIC DU MIDI D'OSSAU

A PRIMULA GROWING BY THE ROADSIDE IN THE PYRENEES

The flora of the Pyrenees is particularly rich and includes some flowers native to North Africa.

CLIMBING ON WINTOUR'S
LEAP

This popular limestone crag,
which is situated in the Wye
Valley not far from Chepstow,
has some of the finest climbing
in the south of England, with
routes of all grades. The climbs
are quite long, as you can see
in the photograph; the climber
– the tiny figure half an inch
from the bottom of the shot – is
already 100 feet or more off the
ground.

CHAPTER THIRTEEN

The hills of home

It is difficult to know where to start when you are trying to convey some idea of the appeal and scope of mountaineering. Trips to the Alps are, for most of us, rather special events that happen once a year and that tend to leave very definite impressions. At home, climbing and hillwalking are fitted into our lives in all sorts of ways, from the weekend dash up to do a snow gully on Ben Nevis to the whole holiday devoted to polishing off a few more Munros or ticking off more hard climbs at Tremadoc.

What does immediately strike me, when I look back on all the climbing and walking my friends and I have done on our homeland hills and around our coasts, is the extraordinary variety of options. At one end of the scale, you might say, you have the winter climbing in Scotland, which attracts climbers from all over the world; and, at the other end, the 30-foot extreme route on some little gritstone crag in Derbyshire, which has yet to have its second ascent.

Some years ago, I did a few routes with a chap I met at Idwal, in North Wales, and the following summer we bumped into one another again at the foot of the Petits Charmoz, one of the Chamonix Aiguilles, where he had just finished a hard route with an American climber he'd met at the camp-site in Chamonix. Shortly after I got back from the Alps, I went up to the Lakes and called in at Stanage, a popular gritstone crag near Hathersage in Derbyshire, on the way. To my astonishment, who should be walking along the foot of the crag looking for someone to climb with, but the American climber I'd been introduced to in the Alps. When I asked him what on earth had brought him to Stanage, where a 60-foot climb is a long one, he said that he had climbed all over the world and nowhere had he found climbs with such a variety of moves and concentrated interest as at Stanage.

THE AUTHOR TAKING THINGS EASY AT WINTOUR'S LEAP

The River Wye is tidal at this point.

My brief period of post-war climbing, before I settled down to family life, started with a winter trip to Ben Nevis while on demob leave. I was on my own, as the war had scattered my former climbing partners, and I stayed at a forester's cottage in Glen Nevis. One morning, as I was about to set out, the forester urged me to take care, something in his manner suggesting that this was more than a casual warning. So, perhaps a little more cautiously than usual, I set off up the mountain only to learn, a couple of hours into the climb, that all the care in the world won't help if the weather decides to play up. The wind, which up to that point I hadn't particularly noticed, literally picked me up and tossed me into a snowdrift about 30 feet away. The sudden blast seemed to come from nowhere. It was only later that I learned that the last walker to leave the cottage for Ben Nevis had failed to return, and that it was over two months before they found his body.

Worrying though the experience on Ben Nevis was at the time, the wind on the Ben that day was nothing like as strong as the blasts Ron McGregor and I were to encounter one winter's day on Moel Siabod in Snowdonia. Moel Siabod is not a particularly high hill – less than 3,000 feet, in fact – and, for a change, we decided to climb it by one of the less popular routes – up the east side, past a lake, then up a broad buttress to the summit. As we approached the lake, the dense spume being torn from the surface of the water hinted at what lay ahead. Foolishly, I decided it was worth a photograph and I had barely lifted the camera to my eye when my rucksack, which must have weighed a good ten pounds, was picked up by the wind and, partly airborne and partly rolling, carried towards the lake. Running as fast as I could, I only just managed to save it.

Climbing up the broad buttress above the lake was easy enough at first, but as we gained height we were increasingly buffeted by the wind and at one point I was knocked off balance altogether and sent stumbling across the ridge. Descending, we felt, was not an option as this would make us even more vulnerable, and so we carried on upwards. As the angle eased off towards the summit, the wind became stronger still and we had to crawl on all fours until we eventually reached the trig point, where we stayed for the next half an hour, lying prone and hanging on to the plinth. Even when the wind eased and we began to make our way downhill, we had to crouch, and we must have descended a good 200 yards before we were able to straighten up and get back on our feet again. I've only been up Moel Siabod once since that day; this time the weather made amends and we were able to keep to the high ground, enjoying the view of The Snowdon Horseshoe the whole way.

The Snowdon Horseshoe is a semi-circular ring of peaks and ridges of outstanding appeal and beauty and, seen from the lakeside just beyond Capel Curig, must surely rank among the finest mountain panoramas in Europe. I don't for one moment claim that it can match the classic Alpine views for sheer magnificence, but its composition and subtle colouring would be hard to equal.

I first did The Horseshoe in my teens (see Chapter Two, page 15) and did it last a few weeks after my eightieth birthday. It is a superb mountain excursion: compact, with fine views all the way around; and offering great variety, from the routine uphill slog to very airy scrambling. But it needs care. Some very experienced climbers have come to grief on The Horseshoe and not necessarily on the Crib Goch Ridge, where the dangers are very obvious. It is easy to overlook the difficulty of arresting even the simplest slip on steep ground.

DOLLY MIXTURE ON THE FIRST
ASCENT OF 'LEG PULL' (EXTREME 13)
AT WINTOUR'S LEAP

SPRING ON THE SNOWDON HORSESHOE

The hill in shadow is Crib Goch and The Pinnacles
are clearly discernible. The stretch from the summit
of Crib Goch to The Pinnacles is the most serious
section of The Horseshoe.

ON THE SNOWDON HORSESHOE

This was one of the helicopters which kept me company as I did The Horseshoe solo one winter's day.

I began to think about what was involved after a stumble coming down a path in the Brecon Beacons one day. We were moving fast, aiming to fit in another peak before setting off for home when my right heel caught a stone and I went flying, completely out of control. Even a minor stumble causes the upper body to be thrown forward to some extent and, unless this is checked instantly, you soon lose control of your legs in the uncoordinated attempt to arrest what can quickly become a fall. In the previous week, I'd been walking in the Dolomites, where the paths are often very steep and stony, and I thanked my lucky stars that the stumble hadn't happened there. Another cause of falls on mountain walks is stepping down on to shale which appears to be deep enough to take at least the heel of the boot but is actually nothing more than a thin covering on a tilted slab. If you are coming off the top of Snowdon and making for Lliwedd, there are several stretches where this is a real hazard.

Over the years, I've come across some very odd things on The Horseshoe. On one occasion, two of us arrived at the top of Crib Goch to find a bunch of schoolchildren strung out along the ridge, with one very worried leader who thought he was on the Pyg track. More bizarre still was the experience of a friend of mine who was doing The Horseshoe one day, starting at Lliwedd, when he spotted – on the Crib Goch section of the ridge, close to The Pinnacles – a strange-looking piece of machinery. It turned out to be a small helicopter which, having clipped the ridge, was so precariously balanced that it risked falling off the ridge any minute. Understandably, the passengers were too frightened to move. At Pen-y-Pass, the emergency services were alerted, and the fire service was first on the scene. Apparently, the firemen didn't take too kindly to the suggestion that they went back and got a longer ladder.

I once had the company of a helicopter for most of the way around The Horseshoe. It was a winter's day and I was on my own, making my way up Crib Goch, when the pilot spotted me and moved in, rather too close for comfort. I'd experienced something like this before, on the Triftjigrat route on the Breithorn (see Chapter Six, page 51), and it isn't at all pleasant to have a helicopter nudging your elbow while you are climbing. Occasionally, as I worked my way around The Horseshoe, the helicopter buzzed off, but sooner or later it – or a similar machine – would reappear, presumably to keep an eye on me. It was only when I had passed Lliwedd and had begun the descent that it finally left me in peace, and I can only think that the pilot – who, I felt sure, was itching to rescue me – needed one more rescue to get his ticket.

Another mountain excursion in Snowdonia which appeals both to walkers and runners is the round of the Welsh 3,000 Footers. When I did it, there were thought to be 13 peaks in Snowdonia over 3,000 feet, but I believe the surveyors have since decided that a hill in the Carnedds is sufficiently separate from its neighbour to be regarded as a genuine 3,000 footer. It is difficult to say when all 13 peaks were first climbed in a single day, but the idea soon caught the imagination of both climbers and hillwalkers following the publication in 1940 of Thomas Firbank's classic book, *I Bought A Mountain* (G. G. Harrap, 1940), in which he so vividly describes 'their walk', as he likes to call it.

I did the Welsh 3,000 with friends about 30 years ago in under 24 hours, but I must confess that I cheated a bit. On the first day, in just under 12 hours, we covered the Snowdon group and The Glyders, after which we camped for the night under Tryfan. The following morning, my companion decided he'd had enough of 3,000

SNOWDON AND THE OTHER HILLS FORMING THE HORSESHOE
AS SEEN FROM THE ROADSIDE NEAR CAPEL CURIG

A truly magnificent view.

foot peaks, so I finished off the Carnedds on my own, taking about five hours. Not the normal way of doing the Welsh 3,000 but, given my age at the time, I felt I should be allowed to bend the rules a bit.

It is difficult to be precise about the distances and heights involved in the excursion since they depend on the routes taken between peaks, but the general reckoning seems to be that the walker covers about 30 miles and ascends and descends something like 9,000 feet. I suppose the ups and downs alone must be roughly equivalent to climbing Snowdon from Pen-y-Pass four times in a day, and then there is the 30 miles to be fitted in. Even so, when we did it all those years ago, there were groups who set off to do the round, there and back, in a day. The runners, of course, do all the 3,000 Footers before breakfast.

The hills of South Wales, especially the Brecon Beacons and the two groups of Black Mountains, offer excellent hillwalking, and for many people they are nearer home than the mountains of Snowdonia. I remember very vividly the first time I visited the Brecons and climbed Pen y Fan. It was New Year's Day and the snow lay deep on the hills. The sun shone throughout the day and altogether it was a day of mountain magic as the Brecons Beacons look their best under snow, especially when there is sun to show it off. Since then I have seen them in every possible weather condition, mostly pleasant, but now and then there have been reminders that these really are high mountains – such as the day the wind was so strong that we had to crawl across the gap between Pen y Fan and Corn Du on our hand and knees.

FOLLOWING IN HIS GRANDFATHER'S FOOTSTEPS, YOUNG TOM ON THE BRECON BEACONS
We had some splendid walks together, ending the day by camping high up whenever we could.

Carmarthen Fan, which lies some 20 miles or so west of Pen y Fan, is a particular favourite of mine. From here, set back from the main hilly areas of South Wales, you have a great panorama which takes in both the Brecons and the Black Mountains. I've done it several times, the last in midwinter, when there was snow on the high ground. Shortly after we started up the ridge above Llyn y Fan Fach, we noticed we were about to be overtaken by a walker carrying a huge rucksack, and naturally assumed that he must on some multi-day trek and was carrying camping gear. He certainly looked a hardy character because he was stripped to the waist despite a biting wind. When he reached us, which didn't take him long as he was a very powerful walker, we discovered, to our surprise, that he was carrying a paraglider and was apparently planning to take off higher up the ridge. Here, I noticed, he put his shirt back on.

It was the first time I'd seen anyone paragliding in these hills, and to see the chap take off the ridge and then find up an updraught which took him close to the top of Carmarthen Fan – and well above the snow line – was very impressive. I'd always fancied doing a bit of paragliding myself, but none of my friends seemed particularly keen and, given my age at this point, there would probably have been problems over insurance.

Advancing age does have its compensations, however, as I was to discover one day when we were climbing at Stanage. I'd worn out my rock boots, and went into Hathersage to buy a new pair. On the shop counter was a notice offering discounts to members of certain climbing clubs and, as a bit of fun, I asked the assistant

THE VIEW OF PART OF THE MONT BLANC MASSIF AS SEEN FROM
THE AIGUILLES ROUGES AT CHAMONIX

It was close to the spot where the photograph was taken that the two little French girls joined me. They had spotted my bulky rucksack and assumed that it contained a paraglider and that I was about to take off. I was sorry to disappoint them. Mont Blanc is the snow-covered dome at the very top centre of the picture. The summit is about 10,000 feet higher than the roads just discernible at the bottom of the picture. The entrance to the Mont Blanc Tunnel, which links France and Italy, is not far from the roads.

This picture also shows the extent to which the glaciers have shrunk. There are various paintings in Chamonix that show them reaching down to the valley floor. Whether the shrinkage is due to the current phase of global warming or not is debatable, as alpine glaciers have advanced and retreated throughout the centuries and there are passes now under ice over which cattle were once driven.

RICHARD BARRETT ENJOYING HIMSELF ON HELVELLYN

The ridge Richard has just crossed is Striding Edge, a very popular approach to Helvellyn in summer but a serious mountain excursion in winter conditions.

whether there was any discount for octogenarian rock climbers. He disappeared for a moment, before returning to say that he'd been down to see the manager and that I could have a discount of ten per cent!

The amount of paragliding which goes on in the Alps is difficult to imagine and at Chamonix there seem to be gliders in the air most of the time. I must have spent hours on the Aiguilles Rouges watching them soar, with the magnificent panorama of Mont Blanc in the background. I was there one day when two little girls – aged, perhaps, five and eight – appeared and sat down either side of me. I was a bit concerned to say the least because I was on fairly steep ground with my legs dangling over a little cliff, but this didn't seem to worry the children – or, it seems, the parents, who were nowhere to be seen. Then the older girl asked, 'Faites-vous parapente, Monsieur?', and when I replied that I was simply watching the others, they left, obviously disappointed. They had spotted my rather bulky rucksack and thought I was about to take off.

Holidaying in the Lake District is, for many people, a way of life which they pass on from one generation to the next, and it is not difficult to understand why that special combination of hills and lakes we affectionately call 'the Lakes' has a unique attraction. For a number of years, until I started climbing again, I enjoyed many memorable days walking on the Lakeland Fells. It is difficult to pick out, from such an assortment of pleasant recollections, the days I remember best, but the ascent of Bowfell – taking in the Pike o' Blisco and Crinkle Crags – is a memorable excursion, which scenically takes in much of the best of the Lake District. In the summer, it presents no difficulties for the experienced hillwalker, but under winter conditions, with snow and ice on the ridges, both experience and the proper equipment are essential. The last time we did the route, we were told that a girl had slipped while crossing an icy gap on Crinkle Crags and had fallen to her death.

The round of the hills bordering Ennerdale is another fine excursion, a long day certainly, but with Pillar Rock so prominent the miles don't seem to matter. The walking on Fairfield has always been a pleasure but the finest mountain day in this area has to be the ascent of Helvellyn by Striding Edge.

The last time I did the Edge it was in full winter garb, a very serious excursion under those conditions which receives regular publicity so I need not expand on the dangers here. There had only been a few people about throughout the climb and, when I reached the top of Helvellyn, I seemed to be the only living thing there, and it was quite misty, which added to the sense of isolation.

I had just started to make my way down when there was an almighty howl from somewhere close by, but I could see nothing until I happened to look up and there, standing on the top of a rocky bluff, was a foxhound. He was apparently as short of company as I was because he followed me closely most of the way down.

Although Scotland has some excellent rock climbing, and winter climbing that attracts climbers from all around the world, it is probably the hillwalking which brings most people to the Scottish hills. The main attraction is often the Munros, the Scottish mountains of 3,000 feet and over, and there are nearly 300 of them. I am always surprised when I learn how many people have done them or are working their way through the list, many of them travelling hundreds of miles just to get to Scotland in the first place. My old climbing partner Ron McGregor has done the lot, but my own tally is a modest 90 or so, mostly climbed in the course of a hillwalking day which has happened to take them in.

It must be very difficult for someone unfamiliar with the extent and the wildness of the highlands of Scotland to imagine the physical effort involved in climbing all the Munros, never mind the organization and travelling to be done. There must be nearly 150 miles between Ben Hope in the north and the most southerly Munros, and together they cover several thousand square miles.

Although I feel that I have missed something by not climbing more of the Munros, I'm surprised, looking back, by how much hillwalking I've done in Scotland since I first climbed Ben Nevis in 1948. Again, it's difficult to know which of the really good trips to highlight as there have been so many of them. The Isle of Arran has always been a favourite of mine, mainly because you can see the sea from most of the high ground and this, combined with some first- rate ridge walking, makes it rather special. The easy walk up Goatfell is well worthwhile for this reason, and provides fantastic views over hill and loch for much of the way.

The Isle of Jura, not far away, is probably best known for its malt whisky and, or so I've read, for having more Red Deer for its size than anywhere else in Scotland. I can vouch for the quality of the whisky, but not for the size of the deer population. On my first visit with Ron McGregor, our aim was to climb the Paps of Jura as we were steadily ticking off the highest peaks on the main islands off the west coast of Scotland. On the little ferry, which crosses between Islay and Jura, we met a couple of young men from Nottingham who were faced, it turned out, with a bit of a problem. They had secured, as part of their painting and decorating business, a contract to paint a bridge on Jura, but for reasons which we never quite discovered, they didn't know which bridge it was they were to paint. However, being a bright pair and realizing that most of the bridges on the island were stone, they decided they just needed to find the only iron bridge on Jura – not so difficult as it sounds, as there is only one road of any consequence on the island.

The Paps of Jura are a prominent feature of the west coast of Scotland, plainly visible from Arran and from the southern end of Mull, where they give the impression of being gently rounded hills with easy grassy slopes. They are certainly easy enough to climb, but on closer inspection they turned out to be craggier and to possess far more character than we had expected, and it was this – combined with the stunning views all around us – that made our day.

The Isle of Mull, still further north, I remember best for two things: the day Andrew, our younger son, and I climbed Sgurr Dearg; and the extraordinary spectacle we witnessed one day when driving around one of the sea lochs on a family holiday. We had stopped for lunch when we spotted a disturbance on the far side of the loch and, being keen fishermen, we knew that it was caused by mackerel harrying a shoal of small fry of one sort or another. We'd seen it often enough before, but never on this scale. As we watched, the disturbance moved steadily towards us and it soon became apparent that we were looking at the biggest shoal of mackerel we'd ever seen, extending a good quarter of a mile down the loch.

As the fry neared the shore, the mackerel began to harry them in earnest, driving them onto the rocks as they leapt to avoid their pursuers, until the rocks were white with wriggling little fish. We had our fishing rods with us and caught 50 fish in about ten minutes. We took them back to our hotel, but they weren't the least bit interested; salmon and sea trout, yes, but not mackerel, which went to feed the cats.

WINTER WALKING IN SCOTLAND, ABOVE LOCH LAGGAN

We were lucky. There was a lot of dark cloud on the hills to the south, but we had a reasonably
bright day where we were.

THE CIOCH, THE EXTRAORDINARY ROCK FORMATION WHICH STICKS OUT FROM
THE HUGE ROCK WALL TOWERING OVER COIRE LAGAN ON SKYE

Ron and I abseiled off from the point in the photograph where the climber is standing.
Glenbrittle is in the far distance.

The Isle of Rum is a very mountainous little island with one of the best one-day ridge walks in Scotland, the Rum Cuillin ridge. No matter where you are along the walk, your position is superb, with the sea always at your feet and, to the east, much of the finest scenery in Scotland. I did it with fellow members of the Guildford Mountaineering Club, and in those days you had to get prior permission to visit certain parts of the island. We camped within yards of the sea and enjoyed perfect weather throughout our stay so, in every respect, it was a worthwhile trip. I can't recall any section of the ridge where we needed to use a rope, but I do remember that there were bits which involved some exposed scrambling.

Despite the misgivings of the devotees who thought that building the Skye Bridge would take something away from the romantic atmosphere most us of like to associate with the misty isle, Skye has lost little of its appeal. It is true that the bridge has connected the Isle of Skye firmly to the mainland in a physical sense, but if there had to be a bridge I feel that the architects and engineers have served us well. As bridges go, I think it fits in rather well and, having twice sailed under it, I can confirm that it looks very impressive indeed when approached from the sea.

The Cuillin Ridge on Skye is without a doubt one of the finest mountain excursions in Britain, indeed there must be few in Europe to equal it. Again, as with so many Scottish ridges, it has all the qualities that the climber looks for. Not only is the Ridge itself impressive and full of technical interest – for those of us with a head for heights – but the proximity of the sea throughout the traverse adds a dramatic dimension. Standing on the top of Sgurr Alasdair or Sgurr nan Gillean – or, in fact, practically anywhere on the Skye Ridge, with the sea of the Hebrides glistening like polished silver at your feet – leaves an impression which few of those fortunate enough to see it are likely to forget.

So much depends on the light and the weather, and the weather on Skye can be particularly fickle. There are times when the rock on the Ridge seems almost incandescent, and other times when it looks depressingly black. On one May holiday my wife and I spent on Skye, it rained for 14 of the 19 days we were there, and May is generally a good month for weather in Scotland. Then again, I have known times when, for the whole of May or June, there hasn't been a drop of rain on Skye.

The weather's changeability is clearly a major consideration for anyone thinking of doing the traverse of the Cuillin Ridge as it's a long, serious excursion with some fairly difficult rock pitches and extensive stretches of very airy scrambling. Getting the weather right is largely a matter of luck, and I have known climbers who have been going to Skye for years hoping to do the Ridge, and they still haven't got the conditions right. On the other hand, there is my old friend Ron McGregor, who did it first time on a weekend dash up from Edinburgh. At this point, I should confess that, while I've done most of the Skye Ridge – and long stretches of it several times – I've never done the whole Ridge in one go. I've always meant to fit it in, but when the weather has been good I've tended to end up on one of the classic rock climbs in Corrie Lagan, which are some of the best in Britain.

The last time we were on Skye, Ron and I got there using the Island Hopscotch service provided by Caledonian MacBrayne, the company which runs most of the ferry services on the west coast of Scotland.

With one of these tickets, which were very reasonably priced, we were free to hop from island to island on a number of different routes. Our walking tour started at Ardrossan, and we took the ferry across to Brodick on the Isle of Arran; then, after a bit of shopping, we set off up Glen Rosa and finished the day tramping down Glen Sannox. From Sannox, we took the bus to Lochranza, where we spent the night. The following day, we caught the ferry to Claonaig, where we were lucky and got a lift that took us to Kennacraig on West Loch Tarbert. The next morning, we caught the ferry to Oban, calling at Port Askaig on Islay en route.

And so, over the next few days, we worked our way up the west coast of Scotland and out to the Hebrides until we reached Lochmaddy on North Uist, where we hopped across to Uig on Skye. It was a pleasure to be on Skye and, looking forward to seeing the Cuillin again, we were soon heading for Sligachan. The ferry crossings had been a memorable experience, but I think that, for us both, the following day – when we walked from Sligachan to Elgol, crossing the Bad Step on the way – was the most interesting of the trip. The day was a long one, especially as we were getting on a bit – quite a bit, I suppose you might say, as our combined age at the time was nearly 150!

A STRIKING PANORAMA IN THE AUSTRIAN ALPS

TRYFAN

For many devotees to Snowdonian climbing and hillwalking, Tryfan is the ideal mountain. It is striking from every aspect and there are enough rock climbs on its various faces to fill a guidebook. Although rather more serious than many of the hills in Snowdonia, it is also a favourite with hillwalkers. Capel Curig is the nearest village.

CHAPTER FOURTEEN
Classic rock and hard rock

By any sensible standards, rock climbing must surely rank among the oddest of pursuits. After all, who in their right mind would want to shiver on a tiny ledge, possibly in a greasy gully and halfway up a mountain, while the leader spends an hour or more wondering how on earth he is going to do the next move without falling off? It may seem a strange way of enjoying yourself, but you only need to watch children on a climbing-frame to realize that the urge to climb is – for many of us – inbuilt, an observation which inevitably invites the response that sensible people grow out of it. But do they? By 'sensible' standards, climbers have been doing some odd things for much of their lives and I, for one, would be sorry to have missed a minute of it.

Familiarity with the way in which rock climbing originated as a sport can lead to interesting insights into its appeal and development, so let's take a look at how it all started. I think few people familiar with the history of climbing would dispute that rock climbing first became a sport in its own right when alpine climbers began to hone their skills on homeland hills and rocks in preparation for the Alpine season. The odd thing is that so many of the early alpinists were clergymen, eminent scientists and renowned lawyers, successful professionals who you'd think might have better things to do with their time. Were the sciences really significantly advanced by taking a barometer to the top of Mont Blanc at every opportunity? Of course not. This was simply an excuse for climbers to get out on the mountains and enjoy themselves, and it is interesting to note just how quickly they forgot their barometers – which were big, heavy things in those days – when having a good time on the peaks became a respectable pursuit.

The terms 'classic rock' and 'hard rock' which I have used as the heading to this chapter have been part of climbers' jargon for as long as I can remember and it is interesting to see that they were chosen as the titles of

TROUTDALE PINNACLE,
A POPULAR ROUTE IN
BORROWDALE IN THE
LAKE DISTRICT

The climb is graded 'mild
severe'. According to one of
the systems of classification,
the grades above this one – in
increasing order of difficulty
– are 'severe', 'hard severe',
'mild very severe', 'very severe',
'hard very severe' and then
the 'extreme' climbs. These
now range, I'm told, from
'Extreme 1' to 'Extreme 10' or
'Extreme 11'.

THE GREAT PROW, A FAIRLY HARD
CLIMB ON BLAVEN, A MOUNTAIN
ON THE ISLE OF SKYE

I am climbing with Andy Heald, who
is leading. It was on this route that I
was hit by a piece of rock which took
a sizeable chunk out of my climbing
helmet. The climb is nearly 400 feet
long; there was rather more loose rock
about when we were there than you
usually find in Scotland.

two influential books on rock climbing, *Classic Rock* and *Hard Rock* (Granada, 1978 and 1974), which must have given the sport a major boost over the years. The books are full of exciting descriptions of climbs and beautifully illustrated. Broadly, they deal with climbs of outstanding appeal, those of moderate difficulty in *Classic Rock* and the harder routes in *Hard Rock*. A third volume, *Extreme Rock*, dealing with some of the most demanding climbs of all, completes the set.

In reality, climbers tend to refer to climbs of acknowledged excellence as 'classic', whatever their level of difficulty. A useful distinction we do frequently make, however, is between the strenuous climb and the delicate climb, and we tend to favour either one or the other, depending on our temperament and physique. Being small and lightly built, I have tended to go for the delicate routes, where balance and the skilful use of your feet are paramount, especially on the harder delicate routes where handholds of any sort are often hard to find.

The names of the climbs also tell us quite a lot about how the sport developed. The earliest names were often topographical, such North Buttress and Central Gully, which made sense as there were no guidebooks in those days and you first had to locate your climb. Then, as climbing became more respectable and perhaps a little competitive, climbers preferred to attach their names to any new climbs they had just put up, giving us the likes of Walker's Gully and Abraham's Route. After that, the names took an interesting twist and a hint of classicism became evident, as in the Sepulchre, Dives and the Innominate Crack, which wasn't altogether surprising considering the social background of many climbers of that era.

These days, of course, rock climbing is very far from being merely an incidental part of mountaineering, and there are many enthusiasts who have never been on a mountain, preferring instead to climb on sea-cliffs, on the gritstone crags of the Pennines, or indeed on any one of the UK's many fine climbing venues remote from mountains. The Dorset coast, west of Swanage, has miles of fine climbing on the limestone sea-cliffs, and there is enough climbing on the granite sea-cliffs of Cornwall to keep the most ambitious climber occupied for years. Then, inland, Cheddar Gorge, Avon Gorge and the Wye Valley – especially Wintour's Leap, near Chepstow – all offer almost unlimited rock climbing of a very high standard.

While rock climbing may appear to have changed a lot, particularly since the Second World War, it has really only changed insofar as modern equipment has enabled the cragsman to climb harder and harder routes in comparative safety. When I started climbing as a teenager, all you had was a pair of nailed boots, a hemp rope which by modern standards broke on quite a short fall and aged pretty quickly, and a pair of gym shoes – usually referred to as rubbers – which we used on the harder routes if the rock was dry. Even on the very hardest routes, the essential requirements were nothing more than a pair of glove-tight rubbers and a lot of luck. The order of the day was 'the leader doesn't fall', which is not surprising. By contrast, the hard climber putting up a new route these days will 'come off', as they say, several times in an afternoon, using the jamming devices he inserts as he progresses up the climb to arrest each fall.

Social changes have also affected climbing. When I first took up the sport, holidays were, for most people, few and far between – a week, perhaps, and bank holidays if you were lucky – and so, with opportunities to escape

CLIMBING ON ANGLESEY

This climb is A Dream of White Horses, an absolute gem with some taxing moves and in a magnificent position above the waves. You abseil down to the start.

CLIMBING AT TREMADOC

The crag overlooks Traeth Mawr and was at one time a sea-cliff beside a sandy estuary. The pastures built up steadily from silt carried down by the river Glaslyn when Madoc built his dam. The climbing on the various crags at Tremadoc fills a substantial guidebook and is some of the most popular in Snowdonia.

to the hills limited, climbers looked around for suitable local crags. My friends and I were lucky: Not too far away from home – at Helsby, in Cheshire – there was a sandstone crag with some fine routes, even if most of them were rather short. A day at Helsby meant a long bike ride each way, but we were pretty fit so that didn't put us off, and the climbing was worth every mile.

Some of the climbs at Helsby had, I remember, very odd names, including what was probably the hardest route on the crag at the time, Morgue Slab. This was the test piece of the day and I will never forget the day when I finally summoned up the courage to do it: for sheer delicacy, I don't think I've ever climbed anything more demanding. Then there's the longest route on the crag, Undertaker's Buttress, an absolutely first-class route.

On bank holidays in those early days – at Easter, Whitsun and in August – I had two days off, the Sunday and the Monday, which I spent climbing in North Wales whenever I could. In order to make the best use of the time, I caught the night train which got me to Bangor at two minutes past two on the Sunday morning. I'd then do the 10-mile walk to Idwal, the first stretch in the dark, starting with the dreary plod through Bangor town, then the rather eerie wooded stretch up Ogwen Valley to Bethesda. The woods were full of owls in those days and their constant hooting didn't exactly boost my confidence, so it was always a relief to get through Bethesda to the point where the road takes to the open hillside.

By the time Bethesda was behind me it was usually beginning to get light and I began to cheer up when I could make out the quartz band on the flank of Glyder Fawr. Strangely enough, it was on the open stretch of road just past Tyn y Maes, and not in the woods at all, that I had my only real fright: just as dawn was breaking, a khaki-clad figure armed with a rifle leapt over a wall and challenged me. I later found out that he was a member of the local Home Guard who tended to take his duties of safeguarding Nant Ffrancon a little too seriously. It was usually about six o'clock in the morning when I reached Cwm Idwal and pitched my tent, which just gave me time to nip up Tryfan and be down again for breakfast at Idwal's Youth Hostel, where I hoped to find someone to climb with.

It is interesting how some aspects of climbing have changed over the years. In the early days, it was almost a rule that a long walk up to the crag was essential before you tackled a climb of any difficulty. I can almost hear my older climbing partners saying, 'Absolutely essential, loosens you up and all that', and they practiced what they preached: we thought nothing of walking from Idwal to Lliwedd for a day's climbing – up by The Devil's Kitchen, across The Glyders and up the Llanberis Pass.

Lliwedd, with its long routes, was still a popular crag then, and one so steeped in climbing history that you half expected to meet Mallory or Geoffrey Winthrop Young somewhere on the route. These days, you rarely see a party on the mountain, which seems to have acquired a reputation for slatey rock that goes up a good grade in difficulty if wet. There is some truth in this as we discovered once when we were doing Red Wall and the heavens opened.

Considering all that it has to offer, I've done relatively little climbing in the Llanberis Pass, one of the most popular centres today, but of the routes I have done there the most memorable was Cenotaph Corner, the classic route put up by Brown and Belshaw, as we had difficulties with a move near the top. Fortunately, a party walking along the top of the crag, having done their climb, spotted our predicament and we finished the climb on a top rope.

Altogether, I've been up to Clogwyn Du'r Arddu three times, the last time only to find the crag glazed with ice and quite unclimbable. The time before that, we did Pigott's Climb, which is a fantastic route, and the time before that I got into a real pickle abseiling. I'm not even sure that I can remember the name of the first climb, but I think it was Great Slab. What I do remember was that we had just finished the first pitch when the weather changed, and within minutes water was cascading down the hillside in streams powerful enough to carry substantial boulders along with them. The leader decided that there was nothing for it but to abseil off and I was the first to go down.

I can't remember using a sliding safety knot when abseiling before this occasion, but this time I decided to set one up, as the abseil was a long one and – since the wall was steep – there was every chance that I would, for part of the descent, lose contact with the rock face and start spinning around. There are a variety of sliding knots for safeguarding abseils, but essentially they lock if something goes wrong and a load is applied to them. Well, things certainly went wrong for me that day on Clogwyn Du'r Arddu – and it was my own fault because I had made the sliding loop too long.

I had just reached the point where my feet would no longer reach the rock face and was beginning to spin when the safety loop caught in my descendeur and locked solid. For the next twenty minutes, with my companions out of sight and oblivious to my plight, I hung on to the rope with my left hand and sorted out the tangle with my right hand and my teeth – all the time gently spinning around on the end of 100 feet of rope. I once saw a similar thing happen to a French climber abseiling off a route on the Aiguilles Rouges above Chamonix, and there was one climber, I heard, who lost his life when his exceptionally long hair got caught in the descendeur.

The rock climbing on the crags around Llyn Idwal and on nearby Tryfan is some of the finest in North Wales, and Idwal Slabs and the main routes up the buttresses of Tryfan are, understandably, some of the most popular routes in the UK. In a somewhat higher category of difficulty than these are two climbs on Tryfan which I had on the list for nearly 40 years before I eventually did them: Munich and Bellevue Bastion.

Apart from its technical interest, Munich is noteworthy for the circumstances surrounding its first ascent which, as one might guess from the name, was put up by German climbers. Legend has it that the climb was a challenge to English climbers to match it for difficulty, and was only accomplished with the use of pitons to safeguard some of the more difficult moves. A few weeks later, however, it was climbed by an English party – and without pitons.

I found Munich difficult, but enjoyably rather than intimidatingly so; it was certainly a good climb, and one I particularly savoured as I had waited so long to do it. But it was Bellevue Bastion – which we did next and was perhaps a little harder – that was, for me, the more interesting of the two climbs.

Although you might expect the most enduring memories to be ones of the days spent climbing the more difficult routes, I have never found this to be the case. A touch of the unexpected, on the other hand, certainly helps to ensure a vivid recollection of a climb. I can still clearly recall, for example, a day in the Cairngorms when we had gone up to do a gully in one of the corries. It wasn't a difficult route, but it was winter and the days were short. The first few pitches presented no particular problems apart from ice-glazed rock here and there, but then the gully narrowed, becoming more of a chimney than a gully.

At this point, the climbing was still not particularly difficult, but then the wind got quite a bit stronger and we were soon being showered with small particles of ice which made it impossible to look up, covered up the holds, and made life generally quite unpleasant. It took us a good hour to finish the pitch and move up to a wider part of the gully, by which time we were frozen stiff. The wind, it seems, had been strong enough to dislodge small particles of ice, a substantial amount of which was being funnelled down the gullies.

We emerged from the gully thankful that the difficulties were over, but our relief was short-lived. Soon after we got off the summit plateau, we were engulfed in a total whiteout and the heavy condensation made it quite impossible to make out the natural features or see where the snow ended and a cliff began. We struggled downwards – endlessly, it seemed – probing with our ice-axes for much of the time, until we eventually found the path, by which time it was dark. A whiteout in the Cairngorms is not something you quickly forget.

When my eightieth birthday came along, I felt the occasion called for a little celebration in the mountains, and a number of climbing friends and I met in Snowdonia with the intention of repeating the climb that had got me started as a boy – The Parson's Nose, above Cwm Glas Mawr – followed, if the weather was good, by The Gambit. We kept up the old habit of camping whenever we could, choosing a camp-site near Capel Curig, but in the evenings – in the tradition of the old Sybarite Mountaineering Club – we wined and dined in a hotel in Betws-y-Coed.

Unfortunately, the late October weather was not very good, with heavy cloud and light drizzle at times, and climbs high up in Cwm Glas Mawr would almost certainly have been greasy, so we decided to try Tremadoc. As is often the way, the weather was much better there than in the rest of Snowdonia and, after a brief stop at Eric's Café, we climbed Boo-Boo, a popular route with a fine variety of moves.

After this birthday trip, I continued to climb occasionally for another four years, the last time at Sennen Cove in Cornwall.

CLIMBING AT TREMADOC IN NORTH WALES

The climbs are close to the road and the rock is sound and dries out quickly; there is a handy little café at the foot of the main crag, which is so closely associated with the sport of rock climbing as to be part of mountaineering history.

I'm climbing the last pitch of Boo-Boo, one of the easiest climbs on the crag, shortly after my eightieth birthday during a celebratory visit with some of my climbing partners. The black and white snapshot shows me leading a climb in the Lake District some 62 years earlier. Notice the gear of those early days: no helmet, no harness, a cut-down mac, trousers tucked into stockings, and gym shoes probably from Woolworths. I didn't wear a helmet for the Tremadoc picture. I'd climbed down the top pitch for what was purely a fashion shot.

THE TRE CIME DI LAVAREDO IN THE DOLOMITES ABOVE CORTINA
They offer some of the longest and most demanding rock climbs in the Alps.

THE LADS ON THE CAMP-SITE AT CAPEL CURIG DURING THE CLIMBING TRIP TO
CELEBRATE MY EIGHTIETH BIRTHDAY
(left to right: Derek Vickers, Richard Barrett, Ray O'Neill and Ron McGregor)

CHAPTER FIFTEEN
Sailing days: down to the Mediterranean

It is surprising how often making a casual acquaintance can end up broadening your horizons. Bob Percival and I met when we were fitting out our boats in a boat-yard in Portsmouth Harbour and he came across to see if he could borrow an adjustable spanner. After that, we stopped occasionally for a chat and I began to realize how experienced a yachtsman he was, having sailed a variety of small craft in waters as far afield as Brittany and the Outer Hebrides. Then, as we got to know one another, he began to tell me about his next sailing project and the more I heard about his plans, the more exciting they sounded: the idea was to take his boat down to the Med and spend three or four seasons there, before returning home through the rivers and canals of France.

Inevitably, I began to wonder whether there was any chance of joining him at some stage, as we clearly got on well and had quite a lot in common, Bob having been a keen climber and hillwalker in his younger days. I mentioned to him that I would be available to accompany him across the English Channel if he wished and when Bob welcomed my suggestion we were soon planning the final fitting out of his boat and making the arrangements for our departure. I will always think of the day Bob borrowed that spanner as one of my luckier ones as it was the beginning of our sailing adventures around the Brittany coast to the Bay of Biscay, around Greece – taking in the Peloponnese – and, finally, home through the rivers and canals of France.

Just over a week later, we slipped out of Portsmouth Harbour and were on our way. Bob's boat was a 29-foot Maxi called *Andata*, a name that not only had a good ring to it but was also particularly apt given that the Italian means it had 'been' places. The sail west from Portsmouth is always a pleasure – past Cowes and

Yarmouth, then round The Needles and out across the Channel, watching the Isle of Wight slowly fade into the distance – and it was a particularly exciting experience for us both, for me as I was looking forward to sailing new waters, and especially for Bob, who had so many adventurous days ahead of him.

But our reveries were short-lived as a cutting wind soon got up and had us putting on extra jumpers and donning our oil-skins in preparation for what looked like a chilly night ahead on the long way to Alderney and Bray Harbour. Just how chilly it was going to get we could never have imagined and, by midnight, half an hour at the tiller was all either of us could manage. Throughout the rest of the Mediterranean cruise and the two summers I subsequently spent sailing my own boat off the coasts of Scotland (see Chapter Sixteen, page 139) and Ireland (see Chapter Seventeen, page 159), I never encountered anything as penetratingly cold as that first night, in early summer, in the English Channel.

At first light, we picked up a buoy in Bray Harbour and, after a quick brew, dived into our sleeping bags, for my part still shivering. We slept till lunch-time, then emerged from below to find a glorious Channel Island day which soon brushed away the gloomy recollection of the previous night. The following day, with the weather good and Alderney a wonderful island for walks, we did the complete coastal path and were lucky enough to see a peregrine falcon.

From Bray, we set off for St Peter Port on Guernsey, where we planned to put in at the Marina. The sailing was straightforward enough, but shortly after we left Alderney *Andata* was spun round on her keel by some strange twist in the current, a reminder of the proximity of the Alderney Race which, on spring tides, runs down this stretch of coast like a mill-stream. The tides off this part of the French coast are some of the highest in the world and very powerful.

Considering just how powerful they are, it is not surprising that I was puzzled, some years ago, by something that happened when we were spending the night in my own boat in a little drying out harbour east of Cherbourg. Just as we were mooring, my wallet slipped out of my back pocket and went overboard. Well, that was the last I expected to see of it, as the tide was already beginning to drop and – apart from thinking what a fool I'd been not to button my pocket – there was nothing more I could do. And yet to my surprise, some days after I got home, a small package arrived containing all my belongings, including the banknotes, which had obviously been dried and ironed. The wallet had been found in a rock pool no more than a few miles down the coast from the harbour. How it came to be there, and not carried further out to sea by the powerful tides and lost forever, has puzzled me ever since.

Bob and I found the marina at St Peter Port as busy as ever. After a quick look around the town, we took a bus to the other side of island where we spent the day walking, and trying to decide where to head for next. The French coast to the west of Cherbourg has so many attractive harbours and inlets that it's difficult to know which to choose. Our first thoughts were to head straight for Tréguier, but we eventually decided to visit St Malo on the way. On this occasion, nothing particularly exciting happened there, but Bob and I were to have a very unpleasant experience when we revisited St Malo in my own boat, *Vixen*, some years later.

Bob had particularly wanted to visit Dinan, and for that matter so had I; but for some reason – and I couldn't put my finger on it – I didn't fancy the idea of taking *Vixen* into the Rance and then working our way up the narrow, twisting channel which leads to the town. Throughout the day, my misgivings grew stronger and stronger until I could not shake off the feeling that some misfortune lay ahead and I would have been content just to leave *Vixen* in St Malo and take the bus up to Dinan. None of this would have made sense if I had tried to explain it to Bob, so we joined the queue of boats waiting to enter the lock leading into the Rance.

The lock was busy with an assortment of boats, including a large pleasure steamer laden with sightseers, and when the lock gates opened it was the steamer that was allowed to get away first. While we were waiting – still tied to the lock wall – for the steamer to move off, there was the sudden roar of a powerful engine behind us and before I could turn round a little fishing boat charged into *Vixen*, demolishing the stern rail and causing other significant damage. The owner had been thrown off his feet when his boat surged forward and at the point of ramming *Vixen* it was totally out of control. It was all very frightening at the time, but eventually everything was sorted out – apart from my frayed nerves – and we ended the afternoon with *Vixen* parked in a marina and Bob and I walking up to Dinan.

By contrast, our first visit to St Malo was mercifully uneventful, and we were soon sailing west to Tréguier, a charming little place with a cathedral as fine as any in Brittany. The little harbour looked particularly inviting, I thought, but then so do most of the harbours along this coast. But for all their appeal, somehow I have never felt that any of the Brittany harbours are quite as pretty as Dartmouth or Salcombe.

The next day, we were happy to sail just a few miles down the coast, where I remember the rose-coloured granite outcrops and – I think it was at Ploumanac'h – an interesting narrow passage into the harbour. The coast ahead of us, from Ploumanac'h round to Brest, has some particularly tricky stretches with very heavy tides, especially in the Chanel du Four, where fog can be an additional hazard. As it happened, Bob and I had the easiest possible passage, with the weather and the visibility both perfect, but some years later, sailing with David Moss from Falmouth to Brest in his boat *Black Rose*, we ran into thick fog in the Chanel du Four and had to anchor close inshore by Plage des Blancs Sablons until it cleared.

Safely, then, through the Chanel du Four, Bob and I made for Camaret, a charming little resort famous for its lobsters and the Château de Vauban; and after Camaret we called in at Concarneau which, with its combination of a flourishing fishing port – tuna fishing being a major industry in the area – and a delightful medieval quarter, was one of the most interesting of all our ports of call.

My time aboard *Andata* was fast running out, but we were able to squeeze in one last island visit before we made for Lorient, the port which, for me, would mean the end of the voyage. Bob chose the Île de Groix, and we moored to a buoy in Port-Tudy. The port was busy in a comfortable bustling sort of way and it reminded me of Fowey; and when we walked in the countryside behind the town we could easily have been in Cornwall.

The following day we motored slowly across to Lorient and, with *Andata* safely moored, Bob saw me to the railway station. From Lorient, Bob sailed south, where he eventually joined a friend before taking *Andata*

AN ATTRACTIVE HARBOUR IN GREECE

through the Canal du Midi to the western Mediterranean, where they spent the rest of the summer. Bob and I were not to meet again until August of the following year when I joined him at Brindisi for what turned out to be five weeks of magical sailing round Greece, finally reaching Athens via the Peloponnese.

The trip out to Brindisi is itself a journey I won't easily forget, as something went wrong at every stage but the last one. I'd often been across the Channel on an ordinary ferry and so when I was offered a passage on the Fast Cat – or whatever it was called in those days – I was prepared to try it, just for a change. Unfortunately, it was not my day: the vessel broke down and, by the time we eventually reached France, arriving two hours late, I had missed my connection to Paris.

Once in Paris, I made some enquiries and was told that, if I could get across the city to another station quickly enough, I would be in time to catch a train to Brindisi, arriving early evening. A taxi was the only option, and after a seemingly circuitous – not to mention expensive – taxi-ride, I arrived at the station only to find that the Brindisi train had already departed. Further enquiries revealed that the last train departing for Brindisi that day would not arrive until sometime after midnight and, worse still, that it was some sort of special express for which my ticket was not valid unless I paid a considerable excess. At this stage there seemed little point in quibbling and, once I'd let Bob know my estimated time of arrival, I settled down in my seat, determined to make the best of a bad job and enjoy the journey across country, which was all new to me.

The train arrived punctually at Brindisi but there was no sign of Bob, and I found myself, a few minutes after my arrival, outside a deserted railway station in the early hours of the morning, with the prospect of searching for a little sailing boat in one of the busiest ports in the eastern Mediterranean. I waited there for about half an hour, at which point I decided that the only thing to do was to try to find the marina. I was just leaving the station, feeling rather worn out and my confidence steadily ebbing away after a trying day, when I spotted Bob on the other side of the road. To my relief, the marina was not too far away, and I was soon snugly bedded down in *Andata*.

I remember very little about Brindisi, but our next port of call, Otranto, a few miles down the coast of Italy, was a very attractive place. We didn't linger there, however, as Bob was keen to get across to Corfu and the other Ionian Islands; then, from Corfu, we sailed down towards Prevesa, leaving Paxo to starboard. Progress was slow at first, which was no hardship in such lovely waters, but shortly after lunch a useful breeze got up and it wasn't long before we had to think about arrangements for mooring at Prevesa.

We hadn't been moored long when, snoozing in the cabin, I felt the gentle bump of another boat coming alongside. Shortly afterwards, Bob beckoned me on deck in some excitement. When I asked him what was going on, he said that I would find out soon enough, adding that it was quite obvious that he had got the crewing formula all wrong. Mystified, I arrived on deck where I was astonished to find, lying alongside *Andata*, a magnificent vessel, twice her size and equipped with an equally resplendent skipper and a crew of four scantily-clad young ladies.

Later, in the cabin, Bob asked me what I made of it all and, pulling his leg, I said I felt that it was a little over the top. Bob didn't believe me for a minute, replying, 'You'd better let me have that in writing, you old prude,' and adding that they couldn't be over the top as they were completely topless – something I had not failed to notice.

I happened to be thumbing through a *Collected Works* of Robert Burns at the time, and it occurred to me that it might be fun to reply to Bob's accusation of prudery in verse – with a touch of the Burns voice, if possible – and the result was 'Modern Times: A Scottish Lament'. It is, of course, all tongue-in-cheek, as I enjoyed the spectacle of the Prevesan Nymphs as much as Bob did.

Modern Times: A Scottish Lament

When I was rovin', fancy free,

A lassie's skirt would hide her knee

With something 'kin to modesty.

Now present-generation teens,

New-shaped in high-compression jeans,

Are giving modesty the go

And putting quite a lot on show.

And, recently, still more surprises,

As girls do navel exercises,

And, where their mums demurely stalked,

They take their pelvises for walks.

And so, for all ye winsome lasses,

From sweet sixteen to thirty-pluses,

There is one rule ye maun observe:

Aye, keep some assets in reserve!

Visiting Ithaca, our next port of call, was, for me, the highlight of the cruise as it is a beautiful island and strikingly hilly. Everything about the place is attractive – the bay, the waterfront and the hills – and all come together in a way that makes the place unforgettable. Ithaca has long been associated with Odysseus and identified as the home where his faithful – and patient – wife, Penelope, awaited his return for 20 long years. Apparently, he got held up a bit on his way back from fighting in the Trojan War, enduring adventures – including struggles with monstrous sea creatures and the blandishments of a siren – which have become the stuff of legend. With his record, you might almost say that it was Odysseus who started the fashion for adventure holidays.

From Ithaca, Bob's plan was sail east down the long strait which separates the Peloponnese from the rest of Greece and then take the Corinth Canal to Piraeus. The Canal is quite short – a little over six kilometres – and is relatively narrow, but it is cut through solid rock and in places the canal walls are more than 50 metres high. Although attempts had been made since the earliest days to link the Ionian and the Aegean

Seas, it was not until the end of the nineteenth century that a Greek engineering company successfully completed the task, having taken over from a French company.

While I appreciated that there was a lot to see on the way to the Canal and that the passage through it would, in itself, be a unique experience, it seemed a pity, having come so far, not to sail round the Peloponnese, and when I mentioned this to Bob he said that he'd been thinking the same thing. So, instead of turning east, we sailed south for Zante and then down the Peloponnese coast to the magnificent natural harbour at Pylos.

Sailing into the harbour was exciting, and the impressive limestone cliffs close at hand reminded me of the western approaches to the Isle of Wight, but on an altogether grander scale. The place was busy with a lot of shipping activity, but the harbour is so vast that it didn't appear at all crowded.

We spent our remaining days in Greek waters cruising leisurely round the Peloponnese and up the coast to Piraeus, with each new day much like the one before: relaxed sailing with the wind tending to freshen in the afternoons. It was an exceptionally hot summer and the heat in the towns was overwhelming; with temperatures rising to unprecedented levels, Greece was, according to reports, struggling to cope with the highest temperatures in Europe. One thing which, to our surprise, didn't like the heat at all was our self-steering control box, which would get more and more erratic the hotter the day became. Once we realized that it misbehaved most after it had been baking in the sun, the remedy was simple and, whenever necessary, we covered it with a face flannel which we moistened from time to time.

Whenever we could, we anchored, and one of the great pleasures of the voyage was relaxing in the evenings, enjoying the sound of music drifting across from some tavern or other and admiring the lights strung out around the bay. Of the islands we visited on our last passage north to Piraeus, two – Hydra and Poros – were perhaps the most memorable, the town of Poros being especially appealing with its white houses and contrasting terracotta roofs.

My Greek adventure with Bob was now almost at an end as I was due to leave *Andata* at Piraeus, after which I had planned to have a look at the Julian Alps, particularly Triglav. The excessive heat persisted, however, and made me think that it might be more sensible to make for the higher snowy mountains of the Central Alps, which is what I eventually did (see Chapter Ten, page 81). It was a fortunate decision as I managed to climb five worthwhile peaks in the short time I was there.

Piraeus was an attractive harbour and, while I couldn't spend long there as I was due to catch the night train, I had enough time to take a look at some of the magnificent sailing vessels berthed in the port. Neither Bob nor I had ever seen so many splendid craft in one place. Bob then saw me, once again, to the railway station where we parted somewhat sadly, having enjoyed immensely both one another's company and some rather superb sailing.

After I'd left *Andata*, Bob sailed her across to the Cyclades where he was joined by friends, and towards the end of the season he carried on to Turkey. The following year, he sailed her single-handed back to the River Rhône in France, and I joined him at Avignon where I found the boat tucked away in a little marina near the celebrated bridge, the Pont d'Avignon. Our plan now was to motor up the rivers and canals of France until

THE MOST STRIKING OF THE MANY FINE YACHTS IN THE HARBOUR AT PIRAEUS

THE BRIDGE AT AVIGNON, CELEBRATED IN SONG AND COUNTLESS PHOTOGRAPHS
It was here that I joined Bob Percival in his boat *Andata* and we set off for home through the rivers and canals of France. Bob had sailed *Andata* single-handed from Turkey.

ONE OF THE MANY HANDSOME TOWNS WE PASSED ON OUR WAY UP THE
RIVERS OF FRANCE

A TYPICALLY PLEASING STRETCH OF CANAL IN CENTRAL FRANCE
Mooring would often involve nothing more than tying to convenient trees.

we reached the River Seine, east of Paris, and then carry on down the Seine to Le Havre before crossing the English Channel. In many ways, this last stretch promised to be the most interesting part of the three year voyage and in many respects it was indeed the most memorable.

For five weeks we made our leisurely way through France, some days covering no more than 20 miles, some days not even that if there was something special to see, as we could stop more or less where we wished and in the canals this often involved nothing more than tying to a tree. Then there was the excitement of all the locks, and we passed through over 200 of them, from the giants on the Rhône – which have the capacity to take large merchant vessels and may be the best part of 100 feet deep – to the sort of lock we are familiar with on our canals back in the UK. While the waterways themselves were very quiet – except near the big cities such as Lyon, Paris and Rouen – we often had to do no more than walk a few yards to find ourselves near the centre of one of those pleasant little country towns for which France is so celebrated, such as Tournon sur Rhône.

The passage up the Rhône from Avignon to Lyon is only possible in a small boat for a short period in the year. The Rhône is one of the major French rivers and drains a huge catchment area, including a large part of the Alps, so that for much of the year its currents are far too strong for a small sailing boat with limited engine power to make any headway. It was partly down to luck and partly because of Bob's careful enquiries that we got the timing more or less right and were never too handicapped by the strength of the current.

After a morning looking round Avignon and admiring the Papal Palace, we cast off and started the long journey home. I couldn't possibly describe all the delightful spots we visited within the compass of this book, so I will confine myself to mentioning a few which particularly stood out for me. La Voulte-sur-Rhône, for example, may not have that touch of rare beauty which makes some of the better known towns, such as Tournon, so attractive, but I liked it nonetheless and I greatly enjoyed our walk around the château, with its fine views down the Rhône Valley.

Tournon itself is, of course, a delightful small town with a fifteenth-century château, a number of striking houses, and the added attractions of a fine suspension bridge and the rows and rows of vines which decorate the hillside. And we spent a whole day looking round Vienne only to realise that we were merely catching a glimpse of its treasures, as the town has many interesting churches and a surprising number of relics of Imperial Rome. What little I'd seen of Lyon, passing through by road, had never struck me as anything out of the ordinary, so I was surprised to note how attractive the city appeared seen from the river; but we didn't linger over this stretch as we were anxious to find the entrance to the Saône, a river which was to take us through some of the most scenic country of the whole journey across France.

When I wasn't taking my turn at the tiller, I would often while away the time composing limericks, which has long been a hobby of mine. Bob seemed to find this very amusing and one day he challenged me to write three limericks, each containing a word or words of his choosing. Since I had happened to mention Stac Polly – a rocky little peak in the north-west of Scotland, which some friends of mine had recently climbed – this was his first challenge. The peak's Gaelic name is Stac Pollaidh, but to climbers it is always known as Stac Polly, perhaps with some justification as the region in which it is situated is part of Inverpolly

Forest. Not that this made my task as a writer of limericks any easier, but I agreed to see what I could do, with the following result:

> There was a young climber named Jolly,
>
> Who climbed up a ridge on Stac Polly.
>
> He fell from the top
>
> And, ere he could stop,
>
> He'd fully repented his folly.

The next test was somewhat harder because Bob specified that I had to fit in the name Llandudno Junction, a little township in North Wales. I had a go and this eventually became:

> There was a train driver named Drew,
>
> Who died, as train drivers can do.
>
> At Llandudno Junction
>
> He received extreme unction
>
> And reached Heaven via Chester and Crewe.

The last of the three was by far the hardest of the lot as the words Bob gave me were 'écluse' and 'bollard', the former being the French word for a lock – we were negotiating several of these almost daily – and the latter, of course, a quayside mooring post. I struggled with this one for the best part of the day, until we came to a lock beautifully adorned with flowers, with hanging baskets of petunias even on the lock gates. If this wasn't enough to inspire me the lock keeper certainly was, a beguilingly pretty girl in her mid twenties who I attempted to immortalize in the following lines:

> There was a young lady named Hughes,
>
> Who kept an exclusive écluse.
>
> A sailor named Pollard
>
> Tied up to her bollard,
>
> Then carried her off to Toulouse.

And so, occupying ourselves with literary pursuits and sightseeing, we made our way through the rivers and canals of France until we reached the Seine some miles east of Paris. In Paris, we managed to find our way into a marina near the centre of the city and for the next two days enjoyed ourselves sightseeing, all for a mooring fee of less than £10 a night. The journey through Paris by boat was delightful, and really is a magical way to see the city, as many others were discovering too, judging by how busy the pleasure boats were. Now, and for the first time since we had left Lyon behind, we had to keep a keen look-out for other river craft, and in a way it was nice to have some company as on long stretches of the canals in central France days had gone by when we didn't meet another boat.

Once clear of the suburbs west of Paris, the Seine has some very pleasant reaches, and I especially remember a little marina near Les Andelys where we put in for the night. It is beautifully situated and not far away are the massive ramparts of the Château-Gaillard built by Richard the Lionheart in the twelfth century. There were few boats in the marina, but one in particular caught our attention because it was an unusually sturdy little ship that had obviously travelled a long distance. Indeed, it turned out that the young couple who owned it had sailed it from New Zealand and that their baby had been born on board.

Rouen, our next port of call, is famous for its churches and, having had a good look around, we turned our attention to more practical matters, in particular to re-stepping the mast, which had been stowed along the deck since we left Avignon. We decided to tackle the job ourselves and, though it turned out to be more difficult than we had anticipated, we got the mast up eventually and set off for Le Havre on the last leg of our journey across France.

What we saw of Le Havre didn't encourage us to linger and, with a good shipping forecast, we decided to cross the Channel that night. It was a glorious night and we seemed hardly to have lost the coastal lights of France before we picked up the loom of the light on St Catherine's Point on the Isle of Wight. Unless you have crossed the Channel at night in a small boat, it is hard to understand quite how moving sighting the English coast can be. Bob and I said goodbye at Bursledon, but happily we were to see each other again before too long – when we sailed my own boat *Vixen* from the South Coast up to the north of Scotland.

A CHEAP BERTH IN PARIS

Andata, moored in a marina close to the centre of the city, and all for less than £10 a night. We made good use of our stay and visited several art galleries, including the Louvre.

UNDER THE BRIDGES IN PARIS, THE EIFFEL TOWER IN THE BACKGROUND

A novel way to see this beautiful city because we were able to take our time, which you can't do if you are a passenger on one of the pleasure boats which buzz up and down the river.

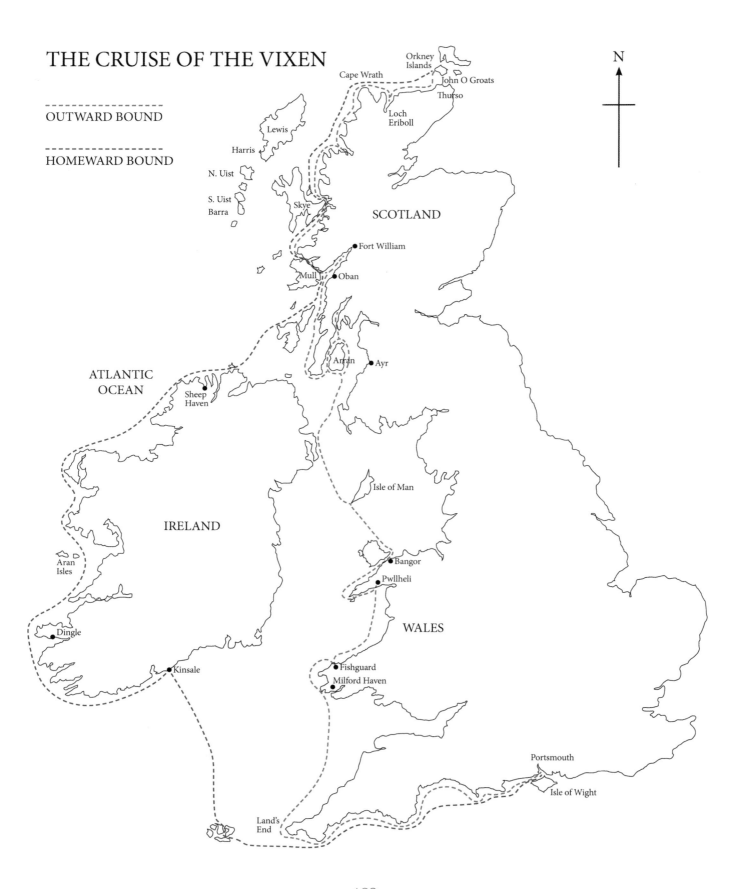

THE CRUISE OF THE VIXEN

- - - - - OUTWARD BOUND

- - - - - HOMEWARD BOUND

N

Orkney Islands
Cape Wrath
John O Groats
Thurso
Loch Eriboll
Lewis
Harris
N. Uist
S. Uist
Barra
Skye
SCOTLAND
Fort William
Mull
Oban
ATLANTIC OCEAN
Arran
Ayr
Sheep Haven
Isle of Man
IRELAND
Bangor
Pwllheli
Aran Isles
WALES
Dingle
Fishguard
Milford Haven
Kinsale
Portsmouth
Isle of Wight
Land's End

CHAPTER SIXTEEN

Vixen goes north: Portsmouth to the Orkney Islands

Ever since my army days when I first sailed a boat off the west coast of Scotland (see Chapter Three, page 25), I had a feeling that one day I would return and sail there again, though I never imagined that it would be something like 50 years later or that the cruise would be quite as ambitious as it turned out to be. Often, when climbing or walking in Scotland, I'd seen boats making their way across to the Western Isles and felt a twinge of envy, but I did nothing about it until one day in Arisaig when Ron McGregor and I bumped into a couple of chaps who had just sailed a boat across from the Isle of Barra in the Outer Hebrides.

Judging by the state of the boat and their account of the trip, they had had a pretty rough passage, but they had obviously enjoyed themselves, and before the evening was out I found myself thinking about the kind of boat I would need for a Scottish cruise. *Wychwood*, my little bilge keeler – though she had taken us safely to Brittany and the Isles of Scilly – was hardly big or sturdy enough for the sort of conditions we could expect to encounter off the west coast of Scotland. Fortune clearly approved of my plans as, within a week of starting to look in earnest, I had found *Vixen*, the 27-foot Marcon Cutlass which was to take us safely from Portsmouth up to Scotland, around Cape Wrath to the Orkney Islands, and home around the west coast of Ireland.

I bought *Vixen* in Exmouth and a friend and I sailed her back to Gosport in Portsmouth Harbour overnight. It was an uneventful trip, apart from a rather rough passage and more shipping than we had expected round Portland Bill, but *Vixen* handled well and the engine, for the short stretches we used it, behaved perfectly.

Three weeks later, in early summer, we set sail for Scotland, the general plan being to make for the Clyde and, after a fortnight or so pottering around Arran and Bute, to return home as quickly as conditions would allow.

For the first leg of the trip, as far as Pwllheli in North Wales, I was joined by a fellow member of my sailing club, Harold Leonard, and after a roughish passage round The Needles we headed for Weymouth, finally anchoring for the night in Portland Harbour.

Early next morning, we took the inner passage around Portland Bill and made for Start Point in Devon. At first, everything was plain sailing, but off Start Point we ran into fog as thick as anything either of us had ever experienced. These are busy waters and can be dangerous in poor visibility, so we decided to try to put into Salcombe, content – for the time being – to anchor in one of the small bays on the approaches to the main harbour. Apparently, we were not the only ones with this in mind because, shortly after we had sorted ourselves out, we heard the rattle of an anchor chain close by. Fortunately, the fog cleared after half an hour or so and we were able to motor up to one of the mooring buoys just off the town, where we spent the night.

The weather forecast for the next few days was not encouraging and we woke up to a blustery morning and a wind which strengthened steadily throughout the afternoon. We were happy to spend a day in Salcombe, however, and took the opportunity to walk out to Bolt Head where we soon realized just how strong the wind was. Although it eased a little the following day, it was still blowing hard enough to make any passage westward a serious undertaking; but we had to be prepared for heavy-weather sailing where we were going, so it seemed sensible to see how *Vixen* behaved in these conditions while we still had a safe haven nearby.

Conditions off Bolt Head were decidedly boisterous and the sight of a small freighter taking aboard some heavy seas gave us an idea of what we were in for. But *Vixen* was handling well and we decided that we could justifiably carry on westwards, a fortunate decision as the wind moderated in the afternoon and we were able to sail on to Falmouth.

The passage the next day, from Falmouth around the Lizard Peninsula is one of the high spots of South Coast sailing and we had a lovely sunny day to show it off, with the wind easing gently as we cruised across Mounts Bay, coming in to anchor off Newlyn. When we left Newlyn early the following morning, the conditions were just what I wanted; I have done a lot of walking and climbing along this coast and I was keen to see some of the crags from the sea, especially Chair Ladder.

Within half an hour of leaving Newlyn, however, the weather changed and a light drizzle quickly became a heavy downpour which eventually eased off only to be replaced by thick fog. For the second time in a week, it descended just where we most needed good visibility, so we went around Land's End without a glimpse of the headland, which was very disappointing indeed as I particularly wanted to see a climb I'd done there from the sea. The fog persisted right across the Bristol Channel, only clearing as we were about to enter Milford Haven early the next morning. Fortunately, although we were to sail *Vixen* for two whole summers – completing a circumnavigation of Ireland and going as far north as the Orkney Islands – we were only troubled by fog on one other occasion, for a brief period off the Isle of Mull.

The passage from Land's End was very taxing and during the long night our only concern had been to get safely across to Pembrokeshire and then dive into our bunks. But it was such a lovely morning as we sailed into Milford Haven, the sun coming out shortly after we dropped anchor in the lovely little harbour at Dale that, after a quick breakfast, we rowed ashore and walked out to St Ann's Head. For the next three weeks, we enjoyed a succession of sunny days which were especially welcome after the treacherous weather of the previous week.

We were away early the next morning and, leaving Skomer Island to starboard, headed for St David's Head, taking in Ramsey Sound on the way. We now felt we had earned an easy day and with a good weather forecast for the foreseeable future we decided, once we were through the Sound, to get as close inshore as safety would allow and see something of this dramatically rocky coast. Off Strumble Head, we cruised about for a while before sailing on and anchoring in Fishguard Bay. The passage the next day across Cardigan Bay to Pwllheli was delightful, with an easy wind and warm sun, and with the mountains of Wales coming into view one by one, first the hills behind Dolgellau and then the whole of the Lleyn Peninsula from Criccieth to Bardsey Island.

THE HARBOUR AT PWLLHELI IN NORTH WALES
We looked in and then sailed further along the coast, finally anchoring at Abersoch.

At Pwllheli, Harold's holiday came to an end and Balfour, another fellow member of our sailing club, joined me. Balfour and I first met when I was working on Vixen and, feeling that he would like a change from sailing across to France, he had agreed to join me as far as the Clyde. I was sorry that Harold had had to cope with such difficult sailing conditions at the beginning of the trip, but he was a seasoned sailor and knew what to expect, and we often sailed together in his boat in subsequent years.

Rather than spend the night in the Marina at Pwllheli, Balfour and I decided to get on our way and anchored at Abersoch, where we were conveniently placed for the passage through Bardsey Sound the next day. The passage was uneventful and the conditions couldn't have been easier, but it didn't take a lot of imagination to appreciate what the Sound might be like in anything approaching a gale force wind.

Since we were planning to cross to Ireland from North Wales, the simplest course would have been to sail direct from Bardsey, but Balfour was keen to see the Menai Straits and I was glad of the opportunity to sail under the bridges at Bangor, especially Telford's fine suspension bridge. Entering the Menai Straits requires care, as the channels tend to change and the navigation buoys can be difficult to spot if the sea is at all rough. There was quite a sea running when we passed Abermenai Point on Anglesey and it was a relief to get into the more sheltered waters leading up to Caernarfon, where we learned that work was being carried out on the Britannia Bridge and that all vessels making for Bangor had to be escorted. This was a blessing in many ways, as the tide races through the narrows by the bridges.

We passed under the bridges early the next morning and even though we had a favourable tide it was obvious that navigating the passage could be a very serious undertaking in adverse conditions. Once under the bridges, the obvious place to make for was Beaumaris, a lovely resort with a fine waterfront and a sturdy castle. We anchored just off the town and had the view of the castle on one hand and the mountains of Snowdonia on the other.

Feeling rather pleased with our progress so far, we decided to call in at the Isle of Man on our way across to Ireland. I had never been there before and I seem to remember Balfour saying that it would be his first visit too. The passage across was one of the most satisfying of the whole cruise, and from the time we left Puffin Island, off Anglesey, to the time we sailed into Port St Mary on the Isle of Man we never once had to adjust the sail.

Of the passage across to Ireland, I vividly recall two things: the sighting of the Mourne Mountains, a hazy soft blue in the afternoon sun; and a huge flock of gannets, which rose off the sea looking, at first, like a giant wave. We spent the night in an idyllic little bay in Strangford Lough before making for Belfast Lough and then on to Larne, our last anchorage before we set sail for Scotland. We were now close to our destination and sooner than we expected we spotted Sanda Island off the Mull of Kintyre. Before long we were feeling our way into Campbeltown Loch, where we decided to have a change from anchoring and instead spent the night in the little marina close by the town. The sail across to Ayr the next day was our last together, as Balfour's holiday was at an end and I had to return home for a few days.

For a fortnight after I returned to Scotland until my old climbing partner Ron McGregor joined me, I sailed single-handed. I put the time to good use, however, sailing up the lovely Loch Fyne and around the Isle of

THE VIEW OF THE MOURNE MOUNTAINS AS WE APPROACHED
STRANGFORD LOCH

Bute before settling for Brodick and Lochranza on the Isle of Arran, both splendid centres for hillwalking. After the strenuous sailing of the past few weeks, I was content to take things easy for a while, which suited Ron because he was a comparative newcomer to sailing, and we spent the time cruising around Bute and hillwalking on Arran.

When Ron left to pursue some studies at the University of Stirling, David Moss joined me. David and I met when, some time previously, I had put a notice on the notice-board of our sailing club indicating that I was available to crew for anyone interested in rather more serious sailing, specifically mentioning Scotland and Ireland. When David responded to my ad, we chose Ireland and had a very satisfactory fortnight's cruising off the South Coast, taking in the Isles of Scilly on the way. This was our first sailing trip together and it led to other interesting cruises, including one which took us down to Falmouth and then direct to Brest on an overnight passage, during which we got entangled in a French fishing fleet and met thick fog in the Chanel du Four.

By this time, the plan I had tentatively sketched out before leaving Portsmouth – to spend a fortnight or so in Scottish waters and then return home – was getting a bit out of shape, and when I decided to over-winter *Vixen* in the Kyles of Bute and spend the following summer cruising up to the north of Scotland, it became unrecognizable. In the words of Shakespeare, there is a tide in the affairs of men, and I decided to take advantage of it, but for the time being I was happy to show David around Arran.

VIXEN SAFELY MOORED IN LOCH FYNE Loch Fyne, which runs south towards the Firth of Clyde, is one of the most attractive lochs in southern Scotland. The principal town, Inverary, lies close to the head of the loch. Otter Ferry, where this photograph was taken, is situated about halfway down the loch on the eastern shore. We went ashore shortly after mooring and had a meal at the Otter Ferry Inn.

The lovely lighting which the photograph captures is not unusual on the west coast of Scotland in May and June and, looking back over the many holidays I've enjoyed there during these months, I can only say that at this particular time of the year the weather is either very dependable or I have been exceptionally lucky. I spent some time on Loch Fyne during the war, learning how to handle landing craft and other small vessels, and there were sizeable shoals of basking sharks in the Loch in those days. Nearly 50 years later, when we spent two summers sailing Scottish waters, we saw only one.

Vixen is a 27-foot Marcon Cutlass, a classic long-keeled cruising yacht. She proved to be a fine seaworthy boat.

We spent our first day pottering about, finally anchoring in Lamlash Bay before going ashore for a meal. On the way back from the pub, we were puzzled to see a large inflatable dinghy cruising around *Vixen* and, when the skipper realised that we were heading for *Vixen* too, he motored across and greeted us warmly. It transpired that he was *Vixen*'s last owner but one and, once aboard, he told us that he had spotted her several times in the previous few days but had never been close enough to be absolutely certain of her identity. He explained that he was the skipper of a whaling research vessel and that they were carrying out certain experiments with their equipment before going further north. He was obviously just as pleased to see his little ship again as I was to learn more of her history.

The cruise round Arran was a splendid foretaste of what we would see the following year, beginning with the lovely view up Glen Sannox into the very heart of the Arran hills. Shortly afterwards, as we rounded the Cock of Arran, the wind got up, and as we crossed to the Kintyre shore where we were planning to anchor in Carradale Bay it was blowing hard. The night was a rough one, the roughest we had spent at anchor so far, but I had paid particular attention to the ground tackle when fitting *Vixen* out for the trip and the holding seemed good. The passage the next day around the south of Arran and up the east coast was classic sailing: the wind was still strong and *Vixen* surged along mile after mile, thoroughly enjoying herself. David certainly seemed to be enjoying himself too as he was at the tiller for most of the day.

The weather, which had been so favourable for weeks, was now showing signs of breaking up and although it was never particularly wet we were beginning to have the odd day of intermittent drizzle. Fortunately, though, it improved for the last few days of my sailing summer, when I was joined by our son Robert and grandson, young Tom, both new to Scottish sailing. It was a great pleasure to introduce them to the Clyde and its lovely lochs, and we made good use of our time together before finally leaving *Vixen* in a little boat-yard at Tighnabruaich on the Kyles of Bute.

During the following winter, I drove up from Hampshire three times to do some maintenance work on *Vixen* and see more of Scotland. The first time I left home shortly after six o'clock in the morning and had rain almost as far north as Carlisle. As I made my way round Glasgow, however, the weather began to improve and when I stopped for tea at Tarbet on Loch Lomond the hills were for the most part clear, though there was still a cloud cap on Ben Lomond. The rest of the drive around the lochs and down to the Kyles of Bute is interesting whatever the weather conditions. Twice, I had late afternoon sunshine and some really memorable light effects on the mountains and another time, on a gloomy afternoon after a spell of very heavy rain, the hillsides were alive with rushing torrents and the valleys awash.

The winter passed quickly as I collected together all the data and charts I would need for the coming summer, the number of charts growing week by week as my plans got more and more ambitious. Bob Percival was with me when I went to collect *Vixen* from the boat-yard in Tighnabruaich. It was a pleasure to see him again, as the last time we had seen one another was when we sailed across the English Channel on our way back from Greece (see Chapter Fifteen, page 125). They had looked after *Vixen* well at the boat-yard and she looked resplendent as she lay at her mooring, 200 yards off shore. We arrived at Tighnabruaich shortly after lunch, but it was blowing so hard that we couldn't get out to the boat in our dinghy, so we made the best of things and went for a walk.

YOUNG TOM AND HIS GRANDFATHER AT TIGHNABRUAICH ON THE KYLES OF BUTE, WHERE *VIXEN* WAS LEFT FOR THE WINTER

The little boatyard there looked after her splendidly.

It was late afternoon when we got aboard and, after sorting things out, we decided to sail down to Ardlamont Point to see what conditions were like in more open waters. The scene, as we approached the Point, left us in no doubt, and we had no choice but to return to our mooring off the boat-yard. Conditions the next morning were far from reassuring, but by noon the wind had died down to the point where we felt that it was worth sticking our noses out. It was still pretty rough off Ardlamont, but the wind eased off noticeably by the time we had Skipness Point abeam and, with confidence returning and *Vixen* handling well, we set sail for Campbeltown.

The passage which we did the next day around the Mull of Kintyre has a formidable reputation and I have known yachtsmen on the round Britain cruise who decided to leave out the surging, rocky waters and take the Crinan Canal. We must have been particularly lucky as we got the conditions just right, and even had time to enjoy the scenery and watch the sea birds.

From the Mull of Kintyre we made for Gigha, where we planned to visit the Achamore Gardens. On the way in, we picked up one of the mooring buoys in Ardminish Bay rather than anchor, as the anchorage here is rather exposed. It was a pleasure to be ashore: the wild flowers were at their best and the island generally had a welcoming air about it. We made our way to the Gardens but hadn't gone very far when the wind freshened considerably and, afraid that we might have difficulty rowing back to the boat, we returned to the harbour where we were met by a strong onshore wind. Bob took the oars, but fit and powerful as he was he had the greatest difficulty in rowing the short distance out to *Vixen* against the wind roaring in from the south-east.

The rest of the day and much of the night that followed were far from comfortable, with *Vixen* being buffeted about continually by heavy seas. Fortunately, the wind died down during the night and, by the time we woke up the next morning, the day looked distinctly promising. After a quick breakfast we were away, as I was eager to see our next anchorage in Lowlandman's Bay on the Isle of Jura. The Bay is beautifully situated on the east side of the island and is overlooked by a number of fine hills, the highest over 2500 feet. It is an extraordinarily isolated place with a distinct feeling of remoteness, a feeling which grew stronger throughout the time we were there as we saw neither person nor boat.

After we'd anchored and generally settled in, I took the dinghy to the northern end of the bay and had just started to row back to *Vixen* when a seal popped up behind the dinghy and began to follow me. For a while there was only the one, but when I began to talk to it and generally make a bit of noise it was joined by several others; more seals continued to join the procession and by the time I reached *Vixen* there must have been a good 50 of them, all following close behind me. It was an extraordinary scene and Bob said that, from his vantage point on *Vixen*, it looked as if I was being followed by a pack of hounds.

From Jura we sailed north, making for Oban and passing by the notorious Gulf or Sound of Corryvrechan on the way. The Sound is a narrow stretch of water between Jura to the south and Scarba to the north, and when the tide is running through the channel at anything approaching its full speed it generates forces which make this one of the most dangerous stretches of water in Europe. Somewhere deep in the middle of the Sound is a huge pinnacle of rock, and when a fast flowing tide hits this obstacle it produces whirlpools and other disturbances sufficiently powerful to wreck sturdy vessels. It was quiet enough when Bob and I passed by, but I have since seen it on a spring tide, when it was an awe-inspiring cauldron of seething water, charged with seemingly unlimited power.

Oban is the principal marine centre of the north-west of Scotland, with ferryboats serving the islands far and near and a busy yachting scene, but the Western Isles were calling so we decided to press on up the Sound of Mull in the hope of reaching Tobermory before dark. The Sound of Mull is one of the most favoured stretches of water on this part of the coast, fairly sheltered for much of the way and with fine mountain scenery on either hand and, as one would expect, it is very popular with yachtsmen. But just as we reached Duart Castle, the wind got up and, suddenly faced with a long, wet passage and no certainty that we would reach Tobermory before dark, we decided to cut our losses and make for Fishnish Bay, before completing the passage to Tobermory the following morning.

Tobermory is a delightful little place renowned for the colourful houses lining the harbour, its congenial pubs and, of course, its setting, as this is the gateway to the Outer Hebrides. And it was the Outer Hebrides that Bob and I had our eye on. We felt that, having come so far, we should finish with a flourish by sailing out to South Uist or Benbecula and possibly doing a bit of hillwalking.

We chose South Uist because it is an island with several fine mountains close to its eastern seaboard but, for some reason or other, the nearer we got to the Outer Hebrides the more aware I was of a feeling of trepidation at what we were taking on. From the time we left Tobermory behind in the early morning to the time we neared the shores of South Uist in the early evening, we didn't see another boat of any description and the sight of South Uist close at hand didn't offer much comfort either. Seen in the evening light, it was undoubtedly beautiful, an island of mountain and moorland, but from a little boat it looked positively daunting. Had there been just a single house in view as we approached it might have felt different, but from the first sighting of the shore to the moment we dropped our anchor deep in one of the lochs, we saw neither house nor person. The next day, when we went ashore and walked across the island, we realized that it was home to a thriving community, but none of this had been apparent as we approached the island from the east.

Our anchorage was in a truly magnificent setting, but the more familiar we became with it the more doubts we had about the advisability of leaving *Vixen* unattended for long. It was just the sort of place where the winds could funnel down from the mountains and, if the anchor dragged, *Vixen* would soon be on the rocks. Although we never fulfilled our wish to climb a mountain on South Uist, we called in at the Isle of Eigg on the way back and climbed the Sgurr of Eigg. It is not a big hill, but it has a strikingly dramatic appearance and commands superb views including, on this occasion, *Vixen* lying at anchor 1,200 feet below.

Bob had time for one more excursion before he went home and he chose the Isle of Iona as he particularly wanted to see the Abbey and the Cathedral. Iona lies just off the extreme south-west corner of the Isle of Mull. It is normally reached by road across Mull and then by ferry from Fionnphort, an interesting little place in its own right. We felt privileged to be able to anchor in the Sound of Iona almost opposite the Cathedral itself.

IONA

Iona is a small island off the coast of Mull where St Columba landed in AD 563. Bob and I visited the Monastery and had a thoroughly enjoyable day exploring the island.

Vixen was anchored a little further down the sound from where the photograph was taken. The following day, shortly after leaving Iona, we ran into a fog bank – the only fog we encountered in two summers sailing in Scottish waters.

FINGAL'S CAVE ON THE ISLE OF STAFFA
The cave is said to have been the inspiration for Mendelssohn's Hebrides Overture.

On our way back to Tobermory, we took the opportunity to have a good look at the Isle of Staffa, and Fingal's Cave, with the strains of Mendelssohn's lively Hebrides Overture ringing inevitably in our ears. We had made a good start to our second summer in Scottish waters and Bob was pleased with what we had accomplished. We kept in touch and, the following year, had some interesting cruising off the Channel Islands and the Brittany coast, but we missed the adventurous sailing we had so enjoyed together in Scotland.

Bob returned home from Oban and, on my own for the next few days, I thought I would visit one or two places close by and fit in a bit of walking. Kerrera, the island immediately opposite Oban, had looked rather attractive as we sailed past and I spent an interesting day exploring the northern end of the island and photographing the wild flowers of which there were a number of the rarer varieties, including some orchids.

I woke up the next morning to a scene which quickly made me abandon any ideas I had of pottering about locally, as there was a brisk sailing breeze from the south-west and every chance of a magnificent day. A brief study of the charts and I was off, with the firm intention of sailing up Loch Linnhe to Fort William and climbing Ben Nevis if the weather held. I was quickly through the Lynn of Lorn and in the more open waters of Loch Linnhe. Linnhe is a very picturesque loch in the grand Scottish manner, especially when you have the lovely hills of Ardgour on your port hand. In fact, the whole scene looked so appealing that it seemed a pity to hurry through it and, after taking some careful soundings, I anchored in Inversanda Bay and had a leisurely lunch. Once through the Corran Narrows, it wasn't long before Fort William came into view and I had to decide where to spend the night. I finally anchored off the Corpach shore, where I hoped to get a good view of Ben Nevis the following morning.

The conditions early the next morning were not particularly encouraging. The mountain was covered in cloud, and even by mid-morning it had only lifted slightly. It would have added some zest to the trip if I had been able to climb the Ben from *Vixen*, but I had been up Ben Nevis several times and there seemed little point in going up again if I was to spend much of the day in cloud. On the way back to Oban, I called in at Port Appin and spent the night moored to one of the hotel buoys; then, after a morning spent walking, I sailed west to Tobermory where I was due to pick up Bert Simmons. Bert was one of the climbers with whom I had spent the second night of my retirement, stuck on a ledge at something over 10,000 feet on one of the Chamonix Aiguilles.

Bert was fairly new to sailing and I was pleased when, after a couple of days sailing in Loch Sunart, he agreed to my suggestion that we should try our luck with the Isle of Barra, one of the most southerly of the Outer Hebrides. The weather was perfect and for much of the day we had the splendid sight of Skye away to the north-east. As we approached Barra, the long chain of islands to the north seemed to glow in the early evening light and I could not help comparing what we were seeing with the sombre conditions Bob and I had met when we sailed across to South Uist just a few days earlier. These long passages out to the far west are always a bit daunting and it was with pleasure and relief that we sailed past Kisimul Castle and entered the busy little harbour of Castlebay. We hadn't seen another vessel, apart from a distant tanker, since we'd left Mull astern.

VIXEN ANCHORED OFF THE ISLE OF EIGG

The anchorage was not as secure as we would have wished but we took advantage of a good weather forecast to nip
up the Sgurr of Eigg, the striking hill behind *Vixen*'s mast.

SUNSET OVER THE ISLE OF RUM

On the way back to Tobermory, we looked in at Canna, which is a popular anchorage with yachtsmen on the west coast of Scotland as there is fine sailing in the vicinity and a number of dramatic anchorages in which you can tuck a little boat if you are bold enough. We hadn't long had our anchor down when another yacht arrived and later in the day we met the crew, a young couple from Sweden who had come through the Caledonian Canal and were on their way to Skye to sample the rock climbing. The trip back to Oban, where I was to change my own crew was uneventful, but I remember feeling that there was still a lot of the north of Scotland that we should take a look at.

Ivan Barnett, my new chief mate, and I had walked, climbed and sailed together for many years, but he was new to Scottish cruising and I thought things looked promising when he didn't pale at my suggestion that we should nip around Cape Wrath and have a brief look at the north coast of Scotland. For me, the new waters began when we sailed up the Sound of Sleat and through the narrow passage of Kyle Rhea, which separates the Isle of Skye from the mainland. The tide can flow through the Kyle like a mill-stream at times and it put on a pretty good show when we were there, though fortunately it was flowing in our direction.

We were now moving into some of the wildest and most remote country in Scotland, country that both Ivan and I knew well, but it was a revelation to see it from the sea, first the Cuillins on Skye and then the even more striking Torridon Hills. Our aim was to reach Lochinver and then to bide our time, as we would need to be sure of a good weather forecast before we ventured round Cape Wrath. The approach to Lochinver was forbidding as it was a gloomy afternoon, but the familiar shape of Suilven, which towers over the loch, helped to cheer us up. We moored in Lochinver, alongside a little pontoon installed to encourage visiting yachtsmen, though it seemed that few were prepared to venture so far north because there was only one other yacht there.

The weather forecast the following morning was disappointing so we spent the day learning what we could about the local conditions, particularly the problems we might encounter between Cape Wrath and Loch Eriboll, where we were planning to anchor. For most of the way up the west coast of Scotland, there are sheltered anchorages which you can make for in bad weather, but on the north coast these are few and far between. Nor is it the sort of place where you might find help in the event of trouble: during the week we sailed these waters, we saw only four other yachts.

At last, we ventured out of Lochinver with a weather forecast that was moderately reassuring and enjoyed a pleasant morning's sailing with enough sun to hide some of the wildness of the coast. As we passed Sandwood Loch, however, the wind got up and the day became decidedly gloomy. Conditions around Cape Wrath were serious enough to make us realize just how vulnerable we were, particularly as a shift of the wind had put us on a lee shore, but *Vixen* was handling well and our confidence in her grew steadily.

From Cape Wrath we had about 15 critical miles to go to reach the comparative safety of Loch Eriboll and it was with some relief that we entered the loch and anchored, laying out all the chain we had: 200 feet of what was, for a little 27-foot yacht, very heavy chain. We spent the evening generally settling in and enjoying the view of the fine hills at the head of the loch, but just before dusk the wind strengthened, charging down the hills in sudden gusts, and *Vixen* was soon snatching at her anchor. Loading the anchor chain to buffer the tension took some time, as *Vixen* was tossing about violently, but we were able, eventually, to stop the snatching. This was vital, as sooner or later the anchor would have dragged and we would have had little chance of saving our boat.

It was still blowing hard when we woke up the next morning and it was tea time before we could safely row ashore and walk to the head of the loch. Despite a rather anxious night, we were confident enough the following morning to venture out of the Loch, if only to see what conditions were like. They were certainly wild, but both Ivan and I felt that they were manageable, so we decided to carry on to Thurso, about 40 miles further east. My only real worry was that we might encounter still bigger seas as we got nearer to the Pentland Firth, but by the time we had Dounreay abeam the seas had moderated slightly and we felt that the most taxing part of the trip was over. Nevertheless, the conditions we faced were still very gloomy, and the sinister bulk of the nuclear power plant close by on our starboard hand did nothing to lighten our mood.

As we sailed into Thurso Bay and made our way to Scrabster, I felt we had been lucky given how narrow the margins of safety had been. At Scrabster, the Harbour Master was on the quayside to welcome us and expressed some surprise on hearing where we had come from; apparently, all the fishing boats which had put out to sea that morning had quickly returned because of the adverse conditions.

The following day, we took things easy and were content with a leisurely walk into Thurso, a pleasing little town with an air of solidity about it. We spent some time chatting with the owners of the only other yacht in Scrabster Harbour, seasoned Scottish sailors who were debating whether to head for the Shetland Islands or sail across to Norway. Somehow or other, a little of their enthusiasm must have rubbed off because the next day we decided to press on a little further north and visit the Orkney Islands.

When thinking about the possibilities open to us once we had rounded Cape Wrath, I'd considered a range of options, including sailing home by the east coast and completing the circumnavigation of Britain, but this would have been such an anticlimax after all the splendid sailing and scenery we'd enjoyed on the west coast of Scotland. Visiting the Orkneys had certainly occurred to me as it would give us a chance of seeing the Old Man of Hoy and I think Ivan had this possibility in mind too.

The Old Man of Hoy is a huge sandstone pillar, nearly 400 feet high, on the coast of the Island of Hoy, and the ascent has been the subject of a number of television spectaculars over the years. Neither Ivan nor I had climbed it, although we had had it on the list, and we were pleased to have a chance to size it up. We were lucky with our crossing as it was a sparklingly clear day and we had no difficulty in picking out the Old Man, which looked even more impressive than we had imagined. After that, we were soon in Stromness Harbour where there were two other yachts: one about the same size as *Vixen*, which had sailed up from the Clyde; the other a splendid vessel about twice her size which belonged to the Cruising Club of Switzerland and was normally berthed in Hamburg.

We were now as far north as time allowed, and the following day we began the homeward journey which was to take us the length of Scotland, around the west coast of Ireland – thereby completing the circumnavigation – and home via the Isles of Scilly. On the way back to Plockton, we put into Kinlochbervie and Loch Gairloch,

VIXEN MOORED AT KINLOCHBERVIE

It was a pleasure to take her picture. She had just brought Ivan Barnett and me safely round Cape Wrath.

THE SKYE BRIDGE PHOTOGRAPHED FROM *VIXEN* SHORTLY BEFORE WE SAILED UNDER IT

and sailed into Loch Torridon as far as we could safely go. This was one of the highlights of the trip for both Ivan and I, as we had climbed and walked on the Torridon Hills on several occasions and were keen to see them from a new angle.

It was fairly late in the evening when we reached Plockton and we anchored well offshore as there were more yachts and fishing boats in the harbour than we had seen for days. Plockton is a lovely little place in a fine West Highland setting and it is very popular with visitors enjoying, as it does, some of the best weather on the west coast of Scotland. It was rather sad to see Ivan depart on his way home the following morning; we had climbed and sailed together for many years and had just shared all the excitement and apprehension of cruising in some of the most hazardous waters in Europe.

Richard Barrett, a fellow member of the Alton Mountaineering Club, joined me at Plockton. He had never sailed in Scotland before, but in the few days he was with me he had the good fortune to get in some fantastic sailing around much of the coast of Skye, visit Canna and to climb Sgurr Alasdair, the highest mountain on the misty isle.

Our first call was Portree, the only town of any size on Skye. There was nothing particularly memorable about the harbour or the town as it was rather a dull evening when we got there, but the scenery as we passed through the Narrows of Raasay was very impressive. From Portree, we decided to take a look at the Cuillin Hills from the classical viewpoint, Loch Scavaig, which is generally regarded, with some justification I feel, as one of the wildest lochs in Scotland. It certainly seems a wild enough place when seen from a little yacht, as the head of the loch is surrounded on three sides by some of the highest hills on Skye and there are vivid accounts of fierce storms raging across the loch which have severely tested yachts which have happened to be anchored there.

I had seen enough of the capricious nature of Loch Scavaig from the surrounding hills to curb any inclination I may have had to anchor in the vicinity. We did, however, go well in towards Loch Coruisk before common sense prevailed and we went about, sailing through Soay Sound into more open water. The day had been sunny since mid-morning and the sailing conditions were now as favourable as one could hope for and yet, on what is probably the most dramatic bit of coast in Scotland, we were the only yacht in sight.

From Soay, we motored into Loch Brittle just to have a peep at Glenbrittle, one of the main climbing centres on Skye and the starting point of many a mountain adventure, but we didn't linger because the sky suddenly became ominously dark and we still had about 15 miles to go before we reached the safety of Loch Harport. We spent the night moored to one of the Talisker Distillery buoys, promising ourselves an easy time and a visit to the distillery the next day. Somehow or other, though, it didn't work out quite as we'd planned as we ended up climbing Sgurr Alasdair by the Great Stone Chute. What better introduction to climbing on Skye for Richard!

The day's excitement was far from over, however, because when we got back to Talisker it was blowing hard up the loch and even though *Vixen* was only yards offshore we simply couldn't row the inflatable dinghy out to her. After three futile attempts we were just about to reconcile ourselves to having to spend the night ashore when I remembered a trick I'd used the previous year in similar conditions in the Menai Straits. We carried the dinghy a good 200 yards up wind and, after launching it, started to row, edging out from the shore whenever we got the chance. As much by luck as good seamanship, we managed eventually to line the dinghy up with *Vixen* and, when we reached her, to hold the dinghy steady while Richard made a grab for *Vixen*'s stern. All in all, it had been a very full day.

The following day, we were reminded once again how variable the weather can be off the west coast of Scotland, especially where there are hills nearby. We were sailing up Loch Harport in what was little more than a light breeze and hadn't got half way across to our next port of call, the Isle of Canna, when the wind freshened, reaching almost gale force strength in the gusts. I was in two minds: whether to make for Canna or whether, given the prevailing conditions, to carry on in more open water until we rounded Ardnamurchan Point, and then head for Tobermory. Had I been less familiar with the approach to Canna I would have gone for Tobermory, but I knew the entrance to Canna well and felt that we could handle any difficulties we might encounter. Nevertheless, it was a relief to round into the little harbour and immediately feel all tension taken off the boat.

Canna is an interesting island, mainly because of the views it provides of the Isle of Rum to the east, and it was a change for us to see so many other yachts now that we were within easy sailing distance of Tobermory. The wind continued to blow hard throughout the night and much of the following day, but there is plenty of enjoyable walking on the island so we made the most of it and were lucky enough to get a brief view of a sea eagle.

The only thing I can remember about the crossing to Tobermory was that the passage round Ardnamurchan Point was not quite as rough as I had expected. From Tobermory, Richard returned home. He had been extraordinarily lucky in being able to combine a very rewarding day's mountaineering on Sgurr Alasdair with some of the most dramatic sailing to be had in British waters. After Richard's departure, I spent a few days exploring Mull single-handed and then made my way back to Oban, where I was to join another old climbing partner of mine, Ray O'Neill, on the final stage of our journey: home around the west coast of Ireland.

THE CLIFFS OF MOHER ON THE WEST COAST OF IRELAND

They are nearly 600 feet high and we kept well off when we sailed past them. This photo was taken on a later walking holiday.

CHAPTER SEVENTEEN

Homeward bound: around the west coast of Ireland

Ray O'Neill joined me in Oban, mid-afternoon, and rather than spend the rest of the day pottering about we decided to get on our way and find somewhere handy where we could anchor for the night, as the weather had a dependable, settled look about it. As it happened, the weather for the next fortnight was some of the most settled of the whole cruise, which was fortunate as the west coast of Ireland is wide open to the Atlantic and prone to occasional storms of extreme violence. I remember the BBC's *Coast* series featured, in an episode about the west coast of Ireland, one headland about 60 feet high that was strewn with boulders. Some of them weighed as much as six tonnes and had apparently been tossed up there by giant waves.

The evening sail down the Firth of Lorn and past the western end of the Sound of Corryvrechan was a delight, but even a couple of miles offshore it was evident that there was some very disturbed water nearby. We anchored in the entrance to Loch Tarbert on Jura, feeling our way in with the last of the light, and left early the next morning as we were keen to catch our first sight of Ireland. When we did eventually sight land, we were surprised to discover how mountainous the countryside immediately behind the coast was.

Shortly after we passed Malin Head, we were overtaken and hailed by an official-looking motor launch. The crew asked us where we had come from and where we were going, and our answers seemed to satisfy them as they immediately did a quick u-turn and shot off in the direction they had come from. It was all rather strange.

We spent our first night in Ireland anchored in Sheephaven Bay and carried on the next day to the Aran Islands, off the coast of County Donegal. Here, we had a strange experience which at first we couldn't account for. On arriving, we motored about a bit, getting the feel of the place, then anchored as close to a small group of fishing boats as we felt we could without running the risk of getting caught up in their ground tackle. We then went below for a bite to eat. Halfway through the meal, we sensed that *Vixen* was moving and went on deck to investigate. To our astonishment, we had drifted halfway across the sound, dragging our anchor with us, and this despite the fact that the anchor was attached to 200 feet of heavy chain and the wind was no stronger than a moderate breeze.

It wasn't until later in the day, when the tide was out, that we discovered what had happened: the sand was so light that you could shuffle your feet through it. We were soon ankle-deep. The sand seemed to be made up largely of ground-up sea shells, which would provide virtually no purchase for an anchor. When we re-anchored and moved in closer to the fishing boats, accepting the risk that our anchor might get caught up in their ground tackle, we had no further trouble, although it blew hard during the night.

Steadily, over the week, we sailed down the coast of Ireland, enjoying a succession of fine days and splendid views of which, perhaps, the most memorable was the view of the mountains of Connemara, or the Twelve Pins as they are known locally. Both Ray and I felt that it would add something to the cruise if we could fit in a mountain, and we anchored in Brandon Bay in the hope of climbing Mount Brandon the following day. But the Bay is very open to the north and we eventually decided that, on this very exposed stretch of coast, we would be foolish to leave *Vixen* unattended while we climbed a mountain.

From Brandon Bay, we sailed west to Sybil Point and the Blasket Islands. The morning started off well, but when we were approaching Slea Head it began to rain and we lost sight of the features – Clogher Rock and Sybil Head – which, for centuries, have been used to guide mariners through this tricky channel. Fortunately, we had our satnav gear to fall back on.

It would be impossible to sail through Blasket Sound without reflecting on the extraordinary success of Blasket Islander Maurice O'Sullivan in describing life in this remote island population to the wider world. Born on the Great Blasket Island in 1904, Maurice O'Sullivan joined fellow Islanders Tomás Ó Criomhthain and Peig Sayers in the Islands' rich literary tradition when he wrote *Twenty Years A-Growing* (Chatto & Windus, 1933). In his book, O'Sullivan tells the story of what it was like to grow up in a place where the way of life belonged to the Middle Ages and the number of times the book has been reprinted in itself bears testament to its popularity. Ray and I saw the Islands in their most benign mood, but it wasn't hard to imagine how difficult life on them must have been when battered by westerly gales for weeks on end.

On the way in to the pleasant little marina at Dingle, where we berthed, we were surprised to see Fungi, the Dingle Dolphin, who had already been a feature of the harbour for several years when we visited, and had become quite a tourist attraction. Another surprise was to find that, although there were two yachts from France berthed there, we were the only boat from England in the marina.

The passage round the south-west corner of Ireland, past the Fastnet Rock and eventually on to Kinsale and across to Cornwall, was pleasant sailing, but we carried with us a keen awareness that these are serious waters where bad weather can quickly turn an enjoyable cruise into a struggle for survival. It was in these

CROMWELL'S CASTLE ON TRESCO IN THE ISLES OF SCILLY

This was the sight which greeted us after a long passage from Kinsale in southern Ireland.

waters that a summer storm struck the yachts taking part in the 1979 Fastnet Race, damaging several vessels and causing considerable loss of life.

Kinsale is a pleasing little town and, for the second time since leaving Oban, we had the luxury of a marina. The marina was busy, once again mostly with the visitors who had sailed across from France, and I felt that the town itself was developing quite a French atmosphere. We didn't linger there, however, as ahead of us lay the longest open sea passage of our sailing adventure since we had left Portsmouth Harbour more than two years previously. Approximately 150 miles of serious offshore sailing separated our snug marina berth in Kinsale from Tresco in the Isles of Scilly and so, at first light, we set sail.

As we sailed down the Old Head of Kinsale, we noticed some freshening of the wind, but it was not until we cleared the headland that we realized just how strong the wind had become. We were in for a long, rough passage. For much of the morning it looked as if we might finish up in Milford Haven rather than the Scillies, but by mid-afternoon the wind had moderated and shifted in our favour, and our confidence in finishing up the cruise as planned steadily returned.

As the day progressed, the weather improved, and the evening was as sunny and as pleasant as any we had enjoyed during the whole summer; at the day's end, we were able to watch the sun go down in the west and, very soon afterwards, a full moon rise in the east. Shortly afterwards, we spotted our only ship of the day, a huge container ship heading south-west. I do enjoy the occasional night crossing, but the feeling of isolation and vulnerability is not easily suppressed, and it was with both pleasure and relief that we reached the Isles of Scilly and made our way into the lovely sound between the islands of Tresco and Bryher.

We spend a day in the Isles of Scilly, which were as attractive as ever, but home was calling and two days later *Vixen* was secure on her mooring in Portsmouth Harbour. The little boat had carried us safely over two summers and for nearly 4,000 miles.

Shortly after I arrived home, having left *Vixen* safely at her mooring in Portsmouth, I received a phone call from a fellow yachtsman, asking me if I would care to help him take his boat around the world. He was planning to take two years over the voyage. I laughed and asked him if he realised how old I was, and he replied that he knew my age and had heard that I was still pretty nimble.

I was delighted to be asked but declined the offer, mainly because I soon get tired of long open sea passages. For me, the attraction of sailing is the entering and leaving of new harbours, and the coastal scenery. When we were sailing around Greece, especially around the Peloponnese, I felt that we were as much on a mountain journey as a sailing expedition, as the country, seen from a mile or two offshore, is enticingly hilly.

As for the future, I always have a plan for some good walking up my sleeve. Have I given up climbing completely? I'm not sure. We were walking on Portland Bill recently and came across some fine-looking slabs; delicate slab climbing was always my favourite kind of route. My rock boots are worn out and I would need some new ones, but then, as you will remember from an earlier chapter, there is a shop in Hathersage which gives 10% discounts to octogenarian rock climbers.

THE OLD HARRY ROCKS NEAR SWANAGE IN DORSET

We anchored close by and had breakfast before making for Portsmouth and home. With all the diversions,
Vixen had sailed nearly 4,000 miles.

THE CIMON DELLA PALA BY DAVID WOODFORD

This truly arresting painting shows one of the most striking of the Dolomite peaks as seen from the top of the Passo di Rolle. The nearest village is the fashionable holiday and ski resort of San Martino di Castrozza.

CHAPTER EIGHTEEN

The appeal of the hills

I touched very briefly on the attraction which hilly country has for so many of us in my Introduction, but the more you try to pin down just what it is that appeals, the more you realise how complex the subject is. Even the 'simple enjoyment of hills', which is one way of summing up the pleasures of hill walking and the more rational aspects of mountaineering, turns out on closer scrutiny to be a complex mixture of experiences which are not always enjoyable at the time. A sunny morning in Borrowdale with Derwentwater shimmering in the distance and the dead bracken all aglow can turn in minutes to a scene of weary desolation as the heavens open and it starts to rain. And such rain. Light drizzle soon turns into a steady downpour. It's too nice a day to bother with the waterproofs when you set off and you are soaked to the skin before you can get back to the car. But, if you have what it takes, sooner or later you will be in the Lake District again, perhaps Langdale this time, steadily becoming more and more appreciative of the hills and dales and often passing your love of the Lakes onto other members of your family. On my desk at this moment is a book which I picked up in a charity shop on the discovery of the Lake District and its attractions. Inside the front cover is a simple dedication: 'To Daddy, thank you for introducing me to these hills.' Simple words, but they say so much.

Right across Britain there are hilly lands of outstanding beauty and hill folk who would never wish to go further than the Lake District, Snowdonia or the Scottish hills. Let's take a quick look at what the mountains mean for the people who choose to walk or climb there, insofar as is apparent from the way they spend their time. The amount of traffic on even the remotest of valley roads in the Lake District on any summer's day is some indication that many are content to see the fells as a passing pageant, varied by an occasional short walk from some car park. Yet they enjoy their modest acquaintance with the hills and dales time and time again, which is what matters. Then there are the fell walkers and the ramblers who choose to stick to the dales; they are possibly the group for whom the hills hold the widest visual appeal. Rather more distant, you may feel, are the extreme rockclimbers who have discovered a crag which might, with a few months' perseverance, yield yet another nigh-on impossible route. Over the years I have met a number of these lads and lassies and I have often found that, beneath the grit and the bold front, there is a deep appreciation of mountain beauty. What is it about romping around mountains that appeals? The physical aspects can be readily appreciated, such as the feeling of well-being that we enjoy after a leisurely amble up to the Idwal Slabs in Snowdonia, or the satisfaction felt by the conqueror of a Himalayan giant once they have recovered from the rigours of the ascent. However, the more subtle nature of the lure of the hills – the aesthetic aspect – is more difficult to define. Clearly a great deal of the attraction lies in the dramatic nature of much mountain scenery; the view of Tryfan in North Wales or the Pillar Rock in the Lake District have an appeal which can often be enhanced by bad weather when, vision-like, they emerge from a sea of mist. It is perhaps the colouring and contour of the hills which we remember best, an outline brushed with green and gold by a symphony of colour is revealed as the sun lights up the head of the Langdale Valley, or the classic view of Snowdon as seen from just beyond Capel Curig.

Although it is the exploits of the hardened mountaineers and rock climbers which get most of the attention from the mountaineering fraternity, it is unquestionably the hillwalkers who make up the bulk of the growing numbers that take to the hills for the sheer pleasure of being there. Wherever you are in our homeland hills, men and women seem to be there in more or less equal numbers. To some extent the urge to climb seems to be born in all of us. How else can you explain the popularity of the climbing frame, now a standard feature in children's playgrounds? If the playground which I and my friends pass on one of our weekly walks is typical, the girls are the keenest participants. Let us look back a little and imagine the young shepherdess living high up some lateral valley in the Alps. It is early summer and she is on the highest pastures tending sheep. The weather is settled and the sheep are grazing contentedly on the fresh grass. Above, the grassy slope steepens until it is capped by a rocky ridge which may seem unclimbable at a casual glance. But the shepherdess has gazed at the scene many times and has noticed the shallow gully which might just provide a way to the top of the ridge. Why, you may ask, should she be interested and why should she wish to climb to the ridge? The answer, surely, is a simple curiosity to see what is on the other side – the force which drives much of our climbing. For the shepherdess, the adventure would reveal what for her was the rest of the world, the neighbouring valley and the village she has heard so much about but would probably never visit – a world just over the ridge but endless miles away by hazardous tracks along the valleys.

Some of the first records of women climbing mountains come from approximately 200 years ago when two very remarkable women climbed Mont Blanc. On 14th July 1808, Marie Paradis, variously described as a peasant girl or housemaid living in Chamonix at the foot of the mountain, made the first ascent. This was an astonishing feat given the prevailing attitude to women venturing on a mountain, quite apart from the physical demands which it placed on the climber and the unreliability of the weather on any high mountain. Mont Blanc is nearly 16,000 feet high. From where she lived, Marie must have seen storms of almost unimaginable fury envelop the mountain from time to time, storms which her instinct must have told her no human being caught out in the open could possibly survive. Mont Blanc had defeated many strong parties before it was first climbed in 1786 by Balmat and Paccard and by 1820 the summit had only been reached 14 times, which gives some indication of its difficulties. Still further evidence of the risks became apparent when, in 1820, a party was overcome by an avalanche and several members were killed.

The next recorded ascent by a woman was made by the wealthy mountain enthusiast, Henriette d' Angeville, in 1838. There has been much speculation about the impulse which drove a woman of Henriette's standing to leave her home comforts and risk everything on what all her friends thought was a completely madcap adventure. Whatever the reasons, she continued to climb for much of her life and embarked on a rigorous training programme before she tackled Mont Blanc.

There were certainly plenty of girls climbing when I took to the hills in the 1930s and my first regular climbing partners were Gordon and Joyce Clatworthy. Gordon had done some climbing in the Alps and, as with many climbers at that time, tended to regard rock climbing on his homeland hills as preparation for more serious stuff in Switzerland, even to the extent of climbing down anything that wasn't too hard. He fitted in traverses whenever he could, which Joyce particularly liked and, I must confess, I rather enjoyed, except on the occasion when we got badly off route on Lliwedd.

On one holiday I was on my own looking for someone to share my rope when, halfway along Heather Terrace on Tryfan, I was overtaken by a girl also with a rope slung round her shoulders but somewhat oddly dressed, I thought, for she was wearing a rather stylish summer frock. However, a chap, who I took to be her companion, soon passed by and since he was carrying a fairly hefty rucksack I assumed that he had the rest of her gear. At the foot of Gashed Crag I encountered the couple again and, after chatting for a while, they asked me if I would like to join them on the climb. I have never tied on more quickly. The girl, whose name I learned was Felicity, soon solved the dress problem simply by tucking her frock into her nether garments, a practice which I later discovered was more common than I had realised. She then tied onto the rope; no harness, helmet or other gear in those days, just the rope round the waist secured by a bowline knot. The climb was a delight, nicely exposed in parts but not too hard except in the chimney near the top, which, I seem to recall, was decidedly strenuous.

Looking back at that day on Tryfan makes me realise how far we have come from the age when women climbers in the Alps and elsewhere were handicapped by the strictest rules of dress. There are accounts of women threatened with stones for daring to set off for the mountains in anything other than the accepted dress of the day, the full length skirt. I was somewhat surprised to find when reading Helen Steven's recent book, *Rising to the Challenge*, how long this sort of dress prejudice persisted in Britain for there is a picture in the book, taken in 1909, of two members of the Ladies Scottish Climbing Club wearing full length skirts on their homeland hills, and on a 50 degree snow slope at that. Apart from getting sodden round the hem, the voluminous skirts added significantly to the difficulties of making effective use of the long ice axes which the ladies were carrying. *Rising to the Challenge* is a lively and very readable account of 'one hundred years of the

Ladies Scottish Climbing Club' with some striking pictures of the members in action and a memorable one of their mountain base, Blackrock Cottage in Glencoe. The lighting in the photograph is simply superb. Another fine picture shows three members snugly bedded down for the night in a snow hole.

Both at home and in the Alps, women climbers quickly took their place alongside the menfolk both as mountaineers and authors of books describing their exploits. As writers they excelled and if I had to choose just one book from the astonishing torrent of mountaineering literature it would be Janet Adam Smith's *Mountain Holidays*. It is a book, like George Borrow's classic *Wild Wales*, to be read over and over again with ever increasing admiration for its author and delight in the tales they tell.

PENNY SMITH ON THE MILESTONE BUTTRESS ON TRYFAN
If I remember correctly, the climb we were on was the Pulpit Route. The lake below
is Llyn Ogwen and the nearest village is Capel Curig, the gateway to Snowdonia.

EPILOGUE

By the time my ninetieth birthday came round in October 2011 I had come to accept that my days of serious mountaineering were over. However, the hills were still there so I planned to see as much of them as possible. I made four trips in 2012, lasting nearly ten weeks in total.

The first trip was to Lake Como. I'd always fancied the Italian lakes in the early spring and they were everything I hoped for: comfortable sunny days, a misty blue lake and a striking panorama of snow-covered hills.

Young Tom, my grandson, accompanied me on one of these holidays and it was a pleasure to discover that he enjoyed walking and the alpine scene as much as I did. On that occasion, having the car and it being Tom's first visit to the Alps, we tended to cover a lot of ground and enjoy the more

Gentian

Soldanelle

ALPINE FLOWERS
Photographed by the author on a recent trip

outstanding viewpoints. I think that what most impressed him was the view from the higher passes south of Barcelonnette.

On my last excursion of 2012 I had two main objectives: to visit a valley in the Ubaye which I had heard was particularly attractive, and to revisit Mont Aiguille which I had climbed some years ago. Mont Aiguille was as striking a peak as I'd remembered, but it was the valley running up from St Paul to Maljasset in the Ubaye which made the deeper impression. A ten-mile stroll down the valley, with shapely hills all around and a magnificent bridge built over the deepest of gorges, rounded off a memorable holiday.

IN THE UBAYE VALLEY

MONT AIGUILLE IN THE VERCORS

THE COL AGNEL ON THE BORDER BETWEEN FRANCE AND ITALY
This was as far as we could go. It was late May and, at nearly 9,000 feet, pretty nippy.

THE VIEW FROM THE TOWN SQUARE IN
THE LOVELY LITTLE RESORT OF SAN CANDIDO

ON THE WAY TO MEGÈVE

MONT VISO
Taken from Ristolas in The Queyras National Park.

LAKE GENEVA
A stunning approach to the Alps

SPRING IN THE MOUNTAINS EAST OF GENEVA

THE DOLOMITES
Early morning from the Auronzo Hut above Cortina

THE DOLOMITES
Not far from the popular ski resort of Cortina

ISLE OF ARRAN
Having spent many memorable days climbing
the hills on The Isle of Arran, I thought the
coastal road would make a change.